THE FALSE COLOR DIVIDE

A peaceful solution to racism.
Arguments over, case closed.

Robert Albert Aymar

Published by Best Seller Publishing®, St. Augustine, FL
Best Seller Publishing® is a registered trademark
Printed in the United States of America.
ISBN: 978-1956649505

For more information, please write:
Best Seller Publishing®
53 Marine Street
St. Augustine, FL 32084
or call 1 (626) 765 9750
Visit us online at: www.BestSellerPublishing.org

Cover Art

On the cover is the artwork of the author, Robert Albert Aymar. It was drawn as an example of gray values by pencil in its first thought of creation. However, over time it has evolved to be so much more.

Shortly after it was drawn, a young man walked up to it and saw what the author/artist had not first seen. It seems that others can interpret things differently due to the way they perceive them. Which of course can be negative and no different from how the world has evolved in racism.

In much of the globe we live on, our humanity has evolved negative views about others based upon the opinions of leaders from the past to the present. The construct of **RED, BLACK, WHITE,** or **YELLOW RACES** of our humanity is false. Just as in the artwork, any other character you see may also not be true. Or is it?

The drawing is of a horse, but many cannot see that. What they see, to the amazement of some others, is a dog. Then there are some who see other things. Interpretations can differ from one of us to another. So is the way of leadership for those who wish to lead us.

Beware of being led wrongly—you may lead all who follow you as falsely as we have been led for centuries, making others in humankind the dogs of your supremacies too.

Special Note

The journey of writing this book has been a great pleasure for me, and I've written it to the best of my abilities. I have poorer language skills in spelling and grammar than I should after so many teachers tried their best to help me. In saying this, I want to thank all teachers who try to teach us knuckleheads to become what you dream some of us may and can become. Thank you all, and never give up—we need you more than you may realize.

I also wish to thank all those who develop the technologies around us today. Without their developments, I probably would not have been able to write all this, because of my lack of skills in the art of writing. In the words of a laborer, there were many times I needed chalk and tape to help cover up my mistakes.

It took me many hours and days to complete this, nonetheless, and I am in debt to my teachers, hardware developers, and influences who have inspired me. The world around us is misleading us up to this day and onward. Most of all, may this honor our God for giving us the grace almost all of us do not deserve. THANK YOU, MY LORD!

I am not sorry for any redundancy in this writing, because the redundancy of racism has gone even further than I have with its false-leading ways.

ACKNOWLEDGEMENTS

Thanks for my first influence in life must go deservingly to my mother, Lieselotte Aymar. In most things, she remained steadfast in her convictions and beliefs. She also led me to believe in the possibility that God is always near, one way or another.

Of course, we live the best we can most of our lives, trying to believe God is real without ever really knowing for sure, until the day God influences us when we need Him most.

For that I thank Him because, in truth, I needed Him more than I realized most of my life. He was there every time I knew of and every time I did not know of too.

Saying that, I must take this moment to give tribute to God Himself: the combination of my mother and Him has taken me beyond many doors that opened, even ones that tried their best to stay closed on me forever. For that I am eternally grateful to my mother and God. With their combined help, I remain a free man, for which I am indebted to you both.

Please note that freedom is much more than not being in a prison cell for life. I have witnessed that the cells of many, and even my own, are the mental cells where we lose faith in our own potential to live without burdens. Because of that, I have lived till today to write to you and others to open your eyes widely and finally end our foolish ignorance of racism today.

There have been many historical influences, good and bad, to have led us this far. As to forgiveness, we must try our best to forgive those bad influences so we may move on. Even if that bad influence is our own selves. I, too, have been guilty of this more than once.

As to our history and the better influences, I give the greatest credit to Martin Luther King, Jr. His dream inspired my own. His dream influenced a greater acceptance of mixing our societies together as one humankind, which in turn gave me two beautiful grandsons, Gregory and Malcolm, who will never be taught by me or anyone that they must bear the weight of our historic past of racism. Nor should they ever be a false color or a color that has been molded to hurt others one way or another.

To them and all children, may we all learn and teach one another that racial divide is racism and is also still a form of segregation.

To my present wife: to this day, Susan, I still love you, but I cannot live with you because our beliefs are nowhere near the same. Sorry, babe, you are not White, only your trained politics and beliefs are—thanks to being led wrongly by institutions whose degrees of learning have not trusted God, science, or the medical facts that truly prove we are wrongfully separating humankind.

TABLE OF CONTENTS

INTRODUCTION

The False Color Divide is about a change that is well overdue. Racism will probably last forever, no matter what course of action we take. However, it would be nice for most of us to finally take a step toward a future of honesty about this divide. From the results of our past influences that have paved the way to the present, it certainly needs to change.

Humankind, since our beginning, has always taught its community that there are differences between one group and another. These differences are only cultural alterations that have become learned behaviors within their own communities. So yes, we are different from one another due to our learned cultural norms.

Even so, this has nothing to do with racial difference or the color of our skin. Let us be honest about that idea and how it evolved, without changing for over 500 years, up to this very day.

A division in the idea of races began in Europe. It may have happened more so in the United States than anywhere else on our planet. Just study our history to formulate your own equation to the truth.

Our American history is a history of migration, even when it comes to our own so-called American Indians in history. We all migrated here. The difference, as some have told us, is that the American Indians migrated here by their own will more than most of our ancestors in the United States have over time. However, I'm sure they, too, had to leave other places for greener pastures.

Our history is a long line of ancestors who left their homelands for reasons that differ, yes. So many left their native soil due to a lack of religious freedom, persecution, exile, or slavery. Thus, we were chased away because of differences in our homelands by our own ancestors.

Now still to this day, we are at odds with one another in a country that claims that we have unity. Yet we still split our country in all manner of ways, including politics and the politics of racial divide.

And now, I implore you to read Chapter 1, which began as an article I wrote. An article that was written to help you come to a conclusion all on your own toward the future. This may help you to decide what course of action you may wish to take. It always pays to be honest with yourself before you can say the truth of what we all see.

1

THE FALSE COLOR DIVIDE

Welcome all to an individual approach for change toward the truth on the division of races. We think we are already very honest, but in truth, perhaps, we may not be so. Most of us have the pride it takes to be honest all the time, on a daily basis in our lives. And for the most part, we do a great job of it as we see it on the surface.

We have a great love for many things in life. But for one reason or another, there is a point where we avoid opposition. In the face of opposition, many of us avoid conflict. Arguments are pointless if you think the outcome will never change. Correct or incorrect, the opinion is individual for us all too. Racism is an issue that many have been and are still very uncomfortable with. Rightfully so, since the conversation began.

Racism, quite frankly, has been a plague upon our planet, which was allegedly stated by African American preacher and current U.S. Senator from Georgia, Raphael Warnock, on public news in a comparison to COVID-19. Yes, racism has been deadly; yes, racism has spread like a disease worldwide; and yes, it was human-made, not God-made. So, one can come to that conclusion, as the preacher did, to make such a profound statement. However, this preacher also plays a great part in the continuing problem of racism, due to also still believing he is Black, as racism has made people believe over time to the present day. Thus, he, too, is another being causing the disease of racism to fester into the future of God's creation, humankind.

Racism has formed itself at present and in the past to create ways to manufacture an arsenal of faults that have seemed unrepairable to date. The evolutionary steps made by the people of our past have shown us that these steps are completely wrong, time and time again. They have given people in our future the wrong information to quench arguments that arise each time they come across these issues.

One of our greatest mistakes is that we allow others to guide us away from the truth even when it is right in our face. Internally, as far as the human body goes, there is no reasonable scientific fact that can or should allow us to divide our Human Race into False Color Divides.

Why should we now finally make a change? For thousands of years, we have allowed leaders to direct us to believe there are differences between us to justify hierarchy, politics, hatred, conquering, supremacy, historical change, and the right to make laws in these regards. Through these mind-sets, leaders have led each of us astray, to divide us with their ingenious so-called intelligence or misguiding imperial rule.

The racial division of the world started evolving approximately five centuries ago. This was done so by leaders of the time who were led by their own counsels of advisors, no different from today. The European culture was thought to be more advanced and modern for its time in comparison to the world they knew around them. To their knowledge, it was. But they were also led to believe they were smarter due to their color difference, which they chose to call White. Of course, now we finally have evolved enough to know that to be untrue. Yet we still use these false colors today.

Hence, we have become fools to their reasoning, not our own. Are we going to continue their will, or ours? The choice is really ours. It is truly beyond reasoning that, as individuals, no one has stood up and made a stand against the False Color Divide to date.

Let us be honest and spend every day looking at each and every person who walks by us each and every day from this day forward. I will guarantee that one thing will hold absolutely true. No one on our planet is one of these four false colors: RED, BLACK, WHITE, or YELLOW!

As long as we keep going this way, allowing others to misrepresent each of us, we will allow racism and its racial divide.

Be as intelligent as you are right now, and look upon this page alone. We see two colors that somehow have been made into so-called races of division. Black and White; are we really?

On this page we see that, sure, it is a white page, and the text is certainly black. However, on a person, do we actually see that? No. But why do we see things that way? Racism!!!

Racism is absolutely wrong.

It is absolutely a lie.

It is absolutely a grab at supremacy.

It is absolutely a crucial reason for a division of the one and only race there is: the Human Race.

This has been a reason for many conquerors to build platforms of leadership against others across our globe. Of course, we can add to it the many other forms of social disruption too. However, we already have gone too far to solve it all in one sweeping mindset.

This leaves us to try the one thing we see by one another's true face value alone—an undeniable truth by sight: the point that we are not these false colors alone in any manner at all.

I am an American by grace of having the blessing of a true American-born father. I am also gifted by other influences. First, I was born in Germany, which gives me another cultural background behind my life's views—in other words, Germany's past history of supremacy, which changed our world almost to a point of destruction. Then there is my German family's side and take on their views as well. Those are my land roots besides a couple other mixed-in nationalities.

Please note that most Americans are native-born in the United States, no matter what so-called color the past has made us, which is really important when it comes to our amazing mixture of world nationalities mixed into one country alone. We are all fellow citizens together.

Then there are the gifts of talent and sight I am blessed to have. These are in many ways the easiest way to see the world because if used properly with honesty, it's hard for someone to pull the wool over my eyes. I am an artist who can see and draw almost exactly what I see. Plus, I have no color blindness to date either. Even so, I can have a difference of an opinion as to shades of color, I'm sure.

Now, science is very factual and should never be argued with religion—which is entirely based on faith. We can also differ due to religion, of course. Even to ourselves, we differ within our minds over the issues. But I, too, have my religious foundation with God, and I will not press upon anyone which way or political stand to take religiously either. On the science end, I will also take a stand for the truth on it as fact. No one is these colors: RED, BLACK, WHITE, or YELLOW.

It is simple as it is. The truth. We are one Human Race that God made in His image. Some of us have continually been trying to stir a pot of hatred since the concept of race emerged. Certainly, this idea does not sound godly in any way; it absolutely sounds human by fault.

For you believers out there, what will you do if when you meet your God, He says to you, What race are you? Please fill out this application for Heaven. Are you going to lie to Him too? Why not? You have been taught that by family, friends, fellow citizens, and tons of historical texts in books around the world that we are these false colors. However, there are no directions in the Bible to answer that, right?

Or are there? For me there are, and that is why I make it my life's mission statement. I fear no opposition on the truth. Nor do I have a desire to fuel the future with any further lies to the world around me that these false races even exist.

Another important element in my life was my learning years. You know that elementary stuff, schooling. We see so many of us take this for granted. Yet we still change everything we have learned because the world tunes us into being the way it has become around us.

I learned many things about the truth in school. Colors were some of the very first things we learned. Those colors are still the same, except when it comes to people. Ignorance has done a really good job at turning the color of people into a lie. As the scholastic years progressed, I learned so much about humankind and ignorance. It still is never-ending, with history repeating itself again and again.

There are two things from those years that still resonate in my mind: the idea of truth and justice for all. Plus, the pledge of being indivisible. I am perplexed by how much we have allowed so many leaders of church and state to guide us away from truth and unity. And then add to it, for us believers, to not believe our religious guide, the Bible, as to what God did when He made us.

I cannot tell you the laws of other countries. However, America has actually allowed us to be false color races, and we accept it. Our applications for jobs ask us to put down this lie in writing, and the company accepts it by application. Never once does the employer consider the employee as a liar because as a country, we have allowed this form of racial divide even by law with a twist. By law, it is written that we cannot be denied on account of race, color, or previous condition.

Now, there is a reason that it is used by employee law—it's the idea of trying to make employers hire a balanced workforce according to a racially nonsegregated work team. Sounds right; however, we still have imbalances, whether we like it or not. One reason is that people tend to work with others who have a common culture to their own, and they do so more because of tradition than race.

It is crazy actually, because this country has had so many racial problems growing up that it is ludicrous that it still continues, even in this manner and by law. I thought we ended segregation, but look, it is still there, because we are still all divided and segregated into false races.

In the year 2020, remember the political circus that passed by us between the elections, COVID-19, and the racial unrest, with supremacy all over the country stirring up issues and current problems. Racial divide is wrong; we are one Race and one planet. However, it continues to magnify as our population grows.

The sooner we accept that it is wrong, the sooner we can lay some of these social-distance issues in the Human Race to rest. Of course, thanks to COVID, keep six feet apart until the cure is made too. But there is no cure for ignorance, is there?

We should have no distance at all when it comes to race because there truly is only one: human. Plus, the idea that our votes really do matter can evolve into a true unity where humankind can lead itself to the possible greater chance for peace on earth.

But this cannot happen with an ever-growing racial divide. Our governments worldwide nurture racial division to file us into categories, as if we need them to. Nevertheless, in truth, they do this to manipulate our misguided learning to win our confidence.

The riots continue, with many protesters also destroying the right to protest with violence, theft, and destructive crime. This will only lead law enforcement and government to counteract the balance needed with mistakes of their own. Crime has its truth too, with or without law. What is wrong never rights another wrong.

So, citizens and law enforcement make mistakes, with both parties losing their credibility, furthering the divide for social unrest. This also increases the now politically described racial Black and White divide beyond reason.

I am blessed to be part of an interracial family, much like many Americans are today. Rightfully so, too, because we are a Human Race in the United States and should always have the freedom to be with whom we love. I have two grandsons who are a mixture of the two main racially divided races, Black and White. Yet that does not make them the next possible false color of gray because they are mixed.

Even though our way has been altered by ignorance, it has been altered too in ways that continue to proliferate hate and racism. Ignorance itself may not be a lie, but if you continue to choose living in it, what else can you call it? Will our future society be at a stalemate forever? Hopefully not, but our next generations need us to evolve before we infect them next.

So-called mixed-race children are placed in a cultural divide of ignorance that sometimes gives them an imbalance that is unfair to them. They are not Black or White by sight in their mirror. But they are by some—if not by many—made to be Black for reasons that are not right either. Nor are they White for reasons that are not right either.

So, until they can stand as they will be, should they deal with an entire historical past that has absolutely nothing to do with them at all? As children are new to our society, and we involved them with an anchor of a past, which seems to be continuing a force that we make relevant: a bad past that is not their own.

Biracial children have faced psychological problems created by our radical racial displacements imposed on them from our misguided ideas. All of our children need to be united with us without lies and contempt against one another.

Personal beliefs and views should not be explained to future generations by those in leadership. These beliefs and views are only personal. They should not automatically be adopted by children, because they should have their own personal beliefs and views. And I certainly hope their thoughts will not be dictated by a law of false terms.

Also, please note that American history is all our history together, not divided. It only got divided because a supremacy made some of us lowly and they needed to be lifted back up where they belong by our sides in AMERICAN HISTORY. The good, the bad, and the truth should be part of our history, to give equal justice on all issues in our history as a nation together, one and all.

This is just a visual note for you to view when you are shopping. Take note when going down a makeup aisle that the spectrum of True Tone makeup foundations are never the false colors of racism: RED, BLACK, WHITE, or YELLOW.

As beings, we are guilty of not correcting this in our country—and worldwide. We are responsible for changing for the sake of our generations to come. Wake up; we must evolve to what we truly are. We are human and every part of the one and only Human Race.

I stand as an individual, indivisible, one Race, one planet, with one and only God. Plus, there is no science that makes these false colors truthful to date. We are racially divided by ignorance alone.

Applications Are Proof of Racism

Evidence that even through applications for basic medical services, we are falsely led to believe we are different by racial division.

Applications are necessary in all kinds of situations for many elements in our daily lives. Because of how I have evolved and because of the research I've been doing these past several years, I have found I can no longer lie on them. Nor do I trust the institutions who are using them.

I do give most institutions, like companies who hire our citizens for our common jobs, some slack for their learned ignorance in having employees fill out applications of employment to fill their workforce in this manner.

Now when it comes to government, every institution for learning, all our fields of medical healing and data, the sciences related to every type of data concerning humankind, and the leaders who are required to know the truth as they say they are looking out for us as citizens, what in the unholy hell are you doing to us as a country overall?

The simple truth has been in the hands of the greatest minds of all leadership far before I made my own discoveries. In saying this, the shame upon your great minds should weigh heavy for all the losses in the world till now. You bastards and bitches have allowed this to go way too far.

I ask our societies to try and forgive those who continue racism in our world. But I also ask each of us to finally evolve beyond this ignorance. And stop racism and the false leading of our fellow citizens in civil disputes over the lies of separate races. Stop the false application where our people are led to lie and believe they are part of some false race that has absolutely no proof of existence.

Special Note

In regard to the photo of an application provided earlier in the chapter, it is a certified document filled out by me to get my booster shot for COVID. As you see on it, I wrote I am Human. However, in many places in our world, we are required to only answer with a lie that we are Black or White to describe who we may be, especially if our citizens do not know their ethnicity.

I very much wish, if you are a citizen who knows no other ethnicity other than the native right you have to be American, that you please do so, and fill it out that you are an American. Or if you wish, you may also join your entire race and fill in Human, as I did.

2

NATIVE OR NAÏVE

So, we are divided. Is this by choice, or is it really learned from the world around us? In other words, are you native or naïve?

Native? When we hear that, it seems to bring up only the American Indian. Who, by some accounts, may have also come to the United States by migration. If so, then they are not really native to America as we have been taught. Of course, they are now, and so you may be too.

There really is a major point to that, and maybe it is high time we explore that concept. We as Americans need to restore our nativity among ourselves.

First, it is very sad to say that there are many in our society who have no idea of their heritage from the foreign lands of their ancestors. However, rest assured we are part of bloodlines from other parts of the world.

The first group of people we think to be natives to the United States are American Indians. They show almost absolutely no past in their own story-telling heritage of the actual place of their origins before America. Why is that? It is not as important as their own nativity here now in teaching their heritage of their own past.

Perhaps this should also be so for all of us today. Our ancestors migrated here for change, and we are running out of places to run. The world is full of places to visit and cultures to experience for those who wish to try—which many people still do, here and abroad.

Of course, that is what our ancestors have done, and that is how we all got here to evolve into one of the most diverse cultures on the planet. So, you're here now, and likely you were born here. If you were born here, you are now American, and it is a native right, meaning that you are, in fact, native.

The indigenous tribes here were native before America was America, which is why you hear some speak of their tribes as being nations, no different than other places around the world. Very much the same as a country, just like any other.

If you do not know your ancestors' origins and were born here, then purely in your own knowledge, you are an American by rights—ergo, a native with an unknown origin, no different than many of the indigenous Native Americans of our land.

More than likely, your ancestors migrated here willfully. Perhaps your ancestors came here to start a new life. Otherwise, they were brought here by means of slavery, asylum, religious persecution, or displacement due to political deportation. No matter how or why they came, you are here now with us all. And your heritage may be part of who you are, thanks to its history and influences.

I know many Americans who never consider themselves native, but they are. So, if we are all native in birth, are we not native by origin of birthright too—if in fact we were born here? Of course you are, and don't be divided as if you are not. Nor should you divide yourselves as a color you are not.

For those of us who are here as half-sons or -daughters of a native, but born elsewhere, we have the right to our new nativity also. If you have been given citizenship because one of your parents married a native, you too can proudly say you are very much given the grace of nativity in the United States, no matter what your other ancestry may be.

Once born here, you began your heritage of being American, and your children to come are born so too. I have two generations of children who now succeed me. They are my offspring and are native, not by grace as in my case, but by birth and roots.

Now, in the U.S., if we were to be called any type of being other than human, perhaps we should really say we are all American by nationality. But our fellow citizens are made to be so many other things before their own nativity. This is because no one here normally is given that as a birthright in a general sense. Thanks to the racist views passed down by supremacist guidelines created in Europe approximately 500 years ago, we are too much else before being our own selves.

Racism is the act of separating oneself from another by differences that, by some type of false teaching, raises or lowers one from another. This false teaching is also not a provable statement or fact by any truthful law or science to date. If it is, it is a law of racist ideals and should be overruled in court in the highest part of our government or any other.

So, if I believe I am White with a thought of pride and even stature, then add to it that I think I am racially different when in fact I am not. Also, to say this when I am clearly not the professed color is downright wrong and a lie. Every part of that whole being has been evolved within and by a lie.

When I buy something white, you can hold it and see the color white; it is not the color of me. Why can I lie and tell anyone I am a color that they cannot see in me? Furthermore, how can a system justify legalization of a law that is written and certify this as a true statement, when it is a lie?

Well, the United States has done so for hundreds of years. There are over 330 million people who live in the United States now under this kind of racism every day without ever questioning its validity at all. This is woven into being racially correct in the lowest court to the highest court of this land. This has also been done in many other parts of our planet too. We have alienated our own humankind around our world.

This is why we should question why racism is so deeply rooted in American culture when we have known all along it was created by those in the past from other lands as a scale to rate us with and by false statements.

The United States has cultivated this like a well farmed crop within the fabric of its society. It is so hard for our politicians to even know which way to turn now that it has corrupted our leadership for this long.

The bloodshed of racism is a long tale, twisted every which way throughout our short history as a nation, and for even longer in other places in the world before us. None of us have found a way out of it since its conception. One can believe this is because of the mistakes of the politics in this nation along with so many others, who also receive counsel from all types of other great guides like the sciences of every field pertaining to humankind and our facts.

Since we formed as a nation, we have had a government that has had to evolve around its nation's voting citizens every election. This is not very easy for those who wish to run for office or manage a platform to get elected to from a group of citizens who brought with them the racism that began in Europe. These groups as they evolved are the very reason for our faults in some way or another.

Racism was not American by design. But it has been refined by our culture in a greater way than any other nation in the world. It has also been publicized around the world more than for any other nation. We have been an open cesspool of the dirt we sling around the world by our or other nations' media networks every day somehow or another. This is a very poor reflection of what we can truly be.

If racism and its design in the United States can be shed once and for all by law, perhaps the world could once again see us as the society we claim to be—FREE.

Of course, it will fester in places forevermore thanks to those who will teach their children or communities poorly—which is the reason for most us to finally, once and for all, try to change it.

We need to teach our children well away from the ideas of supremacy's false teachings. There will of course be resistance from ill-minded leaders in each false-led color. However, once their hold on those who follow slowly deteriorates, they will concede to the truth as we all do when we accept the truth of our wrongs. The same truth will stop our government from being part of it too.

This country has a massive native society that still has not seen its value together. The United States was founded and built to become a union of people. Not a union of labor forces. Not a union of divided state rulings. Nor a union of misguided leaders in government who argue over every

THE FALSE COLOR DIVIDE

issue, divided between parties. The parties of racism still flourish thanks to our division in so many disrespectful manners. Respect is given to those who give respect, not expect it.

Our history has unfolded with many ignoring the truths about our governmental actions. Most of the time, it has been ignored to protect the ideal that we are molding this country beyond the borders of racism. The very start of that can be said by historians to be the Civil War. However, that only began the twist that has still not changed to date.

Abraham Lincoln gets the credit for freeing slaves in American history as the story is told. These people also had to evolve on our soil while growing in numbers by generations of new native inhabitants of the United States. Yet they were not considered to be American at that time. They were only given what the United States then could admit to due to racist ideals of American supremacies of the time. Their enslavement was wrong. Citizens, natives should not be available for ownership.

This may be true in one way; however, there were other important elements going on in our history at the same time. It was a major time for change, and it could not happen in one mind-setting sweep, because racist minds were not willing to give up or give a native right to people they still thought of as less than them.

Freeing thousands of slaves meant a lot of new people in our society needed to fill in where they could. These new citizens had no wealth at that time to speak of to begin their free lives. Plus remember, most Americans of that time came from the racist-created world of Europe. So, these new citizens had no rights other than to be free to still suffer our racism.

They had no stature in the communities other than being lowly workers who still got paid the least in our society. It was very hard for our new fellow Americans to live that way. Many were arrested because they were not given any fair justice, thanks to the prejudice of racism. The new law of the Thirteenth Amendment gave our government the only supreme right to enslave an American, which those of African descent served unjustly all too often.

What? Yes, that is true! It may not be told to you that way because that in itself is still allowing some sort of slavery in the United States. Except now all citizens who break the law can be enslaved. Most so-called Blacks of that time were poor, with no land, and were experiencing unfair treatment thanks to racism. They were the largest portion of the population in American prisons and jails around our biggest cities. These prisoners were the new world of American slavery, legalized by the Thirteenth Amendment.

The Thirteenth Amendment sounds great when you read the first part; however, read the whole thing and see for yourself in the second part, where it gave the right only for government to enslave. This also meant that no longer may a slave be sold in the United States, but yes, our native sons and daughters could be enslaved by their own country's political law, which in the southern states, became a way to keep their part in society down and lesser than other citizens.

The Thirteenth Amendment

The Thirteenth Amendment to the United States Constitution only abolished slavery and involuntary servitude, EXCEPT as punishment for a crime, thereby giving the right to treat a prisoner as a slave when imprisoned by a state or federal institution. And it reads this way.

Section 1

Neither slavery nor involuntary servitude, except as a punishment for a crime whereof the party shall have been duly convicted, shall exist within the United States, or any place subject of their jurisdiction.

So it is by law that we can be made to follow a servitude of slavery by law ever since this amendment was established to the United States Constitution.

This of course has been argued, and changes have evolved since then, but the amendment still exists today. Now we have cleaned it up a little by stating our prisons are now Departments of Corrections. That is a misguided statement in itself for obvious reasons. There is no correction.

No prisoner is truly guided to any correction that will help or guide that individual away from their past life. They are not taught to live without repeating their mistakes. So many recirculate back to the prisons in the United States, which also have had our native so-called **RED, BLACK, WHITE,** or **YELLOW** Americans in it.

When African descendants—now also native Americans—could vote, our government formed ways to prevent them from voting. Remember how no citizen could vote with a criminal conviction evermore once convicted.

They did the math then and did this to make it harder for a so-called Black citizen to get into public office. Many African native American men then had past convictions. Also, many southern cities had large African native American populations too. This worked for many, many years.

However, thanks to President Obama and his administration, felons can now vote once their time has been served. There are some criminals who are still not given the right to vote by law. Even so, this is probably also ignored by some so that these voters are indebted to swing their vote to the political party that provided them voting rights. Voters bought by false freedoms of voting rights. Freedom is not bought or sold in the United States, or is it?

They could have voted when President Trump got elected to his first term for President, yet still many did not. Were they aware of their rights being changed? Many, yes, but even for that first term of President Trump, many still did not. There were some people who did vote. But they voted for Trump because he was very much not a politician in any way yet seen in American history today. To those who did, they thought his uncommon character would be good for our nation and good for them too.

President Trump made many Americans upset with his decisions that became unpopular and look what happened: he lost. Quite frankly, he lost in part of because of that and in part because of the now 33 percent of the African native American adult males who are ex-felons, and now voters, as well as many other types of ethnicities in that new voting power today.[1]

It was a long-awaited move by the Democratic Party to get that voting population, and it proved to work in the 2020 elections. Yet please note, it

[1] Shannon SKS, Uggen C, Schnittker J, Thompson M, Wakefield S, Massoglia M. "The Growth, Scope, and Spatial Distribution of People with Felony Records in the United States, 1948–2010." *Demography*. 2017 Oct;54(5):1795–1818. doi: 10.1007/s13524-017-0611-1. PMID: 28895078; PMCID: PMC5996985.

was also the Democratic Party of the past who stopped these African native American males from voting due to their racism.

Does their racism still exist, or is it really now only their supremacies to manipulate the voting populations to vote their way? I believe it's the latter because now there are rumors and claims of Democrats pushing to give immigrants the right to vote before they have the right to be citizens. If this is true, then now even your native rights are more meaningless. In the future, all of this is fueling platforms of supremacy as well as further division without us even realizing it.

That said, as far as I'm concerned, if any group of people deserve recognition, it should finally go to those who have suffered their own way up in society as they have been our own native inhabitants too. Mind you, those who have been wronged in the past are now gone and deserve their historical recognition, which they do get. However, they should still not be represented as a False Race. It's important to think about it in the sense of what fueled the past to go in the direction it did.

This White Supremacy thing has lasted way too long, especially when it has always been based on misguided facts of intelligence or the power of speech that guided the people of our past. So many arguments and wars have been waged on these falsely guided platforms. Yet now, we are continuing our legacy of racism with the next power continuing the forms of divided races in the United States once again.

The racial platforms need to end, because if not, they will only grow greater and greater with our population growing with it. The idea of differences between us all has been proven over and over again to be not true. The truth is, we are not separate races and only have been seen this way thanks to racism alone. This naïve concept takes away our native rights as Americans overall.

Plus, as the diversified country that we are, we should finally give all our native rights as a single race that is human in the United States. Let us not be naïve about being one country that the whole world has watched evolve now for over two centuries this way. Can we afford to live the racist lie we do any longer? It shows we have not progressed, despite what leaders try to portray.

No one is these colors of the "False Color Divide," nor will we ever be. Nor are we any other ethnicity before our own native right. I may be German American, but I was born in Germany. So yes, Germany can come first as to my origin of birth. How can an American born here be considered their past ethnicity when they are born here as native to this land first? Especially those who do not even know the original country their ancestors are from.

For instance, if I was born here, I would be American German. My nativity is where I am from first. But we have taken our native right of origin away from us. So, the thought that we are something before our own country's origin is laid aside. This too separates a being from their country on top of all the ideas of racial origins.

No society should take away a native right. We are as we are. The place we grow cultivates our thoughts as we grow. If I were a so-called Black man, why should my place of origin be a place in which I know no one, nor do I have a generation of my family that remembers being from there either?

Then, in that thought, I am not an African American at all any longer. By truth, I should consider myself only as I am first in all my own knowledge a native American son with very possible African descent.

Racism is a cruel divider of truth. It takes away a citizen's birthright and sets them in groups they did not choose. It set us in groups of false origins and false colors. Racism places people in a past that no longer should exist. Racism takes away an American dream and freedom that we all deserve. Racism can push us into having guilt for things we cannot process guilt for. Nor of a past we had no part in. Racism is an act of oppression that no citizen deserves.

All guilt belongs to those who form groups that show racial divide. The nativity of our birth is our place of origin. Our race is one kind only. We are all human beings who can understand mistakes and misguiding. May none of us ever be again the racist who disturbs another human's life with hate, disdain, or their own supremacy over another. May more of us each day become the antiracist who changes the world around us forevermore.

3

THE FENCE

The fence! We all know the effect of having one. Its purpose is to divide ourselves from things. However, it becomes more of a way to separate one another on or around our property and create even boundaries we've made in our cultures. We end up using these fences to hang so many of our different opinions that they end up defining us at the end of the day.

The False Color Divide is a very invisible and visible fence! How so? one might ask. Racism is about priority lines and the boundaries that have divided us.

Each and every one of us has our own boundaries that we set within our minds. They vary for each of us based on our personal reasoning. Each and every one of us have different experiences from one another.

Our evolution in racism may have gone on for over 500 years on record, but it began far before that, I am sure. Racism is about differences we are taught from the beginning of our lineage. The False Color Divide did not come first, I can assure you.

Survival is the biggest beginning of our teachings on how to survive. Racism is what evolved thousands of years following that. We can think about the beginnings of it all. However, its history is way too long to cover for this type of reading. Just imagine the divide-and-conquer aspect; to the conqueror goes the spoils. People were and still are today one of the greatest spoils taken advantage of to date.

So where do you or I lie upon this fence? As I said, it's very individual. For me, the fence was always a thing I saw but questioned right from the beginning within my own time and reasoning. Each of us have different experiences in our lives, as is the case with so many past leaders. Leaders who taught each of us how to behave as we do at this very moment.

Since my conception of this theory, I have spoken with everyone who will talk with me on the concept. Trust me, many of us are very embedded with what we believe. As well, I do have friends in different parts of the divide, and I am trying to build these friends into a greater part of change.

Many of us sadly believe and write on applications or reports, even medically, that we are these colors of the False Color Divide. This is what our past learning experiences have programmed us to believe and the way we act. Perhaps this is why we believe that we are a part of a race in the divide with our false color.

Is that the foundation of racism? Of course it is, especially when we are in a group of the same, having some complaint that is against the other among ourselves. We have become the very thing we speak of—voicing disdain within our own groups toward others.

We build our own verbal opinions from learned behaviors, pulling others to carry the banner with us together. This is how leaders of the divide pull our communities deeper into racism than many of us truly wish to go.

Blessed are the few—and there are more than we all individually know—who do not believe in False Races. We do not see ourselves as being part of the color-coded races. Nor do we take part in those kinds of conversations. However, our fence is there because most of us still register ourselves as one of these color races. If I try to speak with another who believes they are any one of these colors, they respond as being in their place of race. That is why it is difficult to help break the False Color Divide.

Nevertheless, slowly the property lines are being broken because of racism's unfounded truths. There are people who have learned over their own time that there is no greater whole in divided races. For their reasons of faith and experience, they see the truth in the mirror. Either you believe in what you see in your own image or you follow the lie of racism.

Racism is not a job; however, a fence is a job that needs tending to. Just like the fence in racism, a believer in faith tends to a fence too. For those who live with faith in religions and yet have their beliefs in racism suffer the greatest price. They have imprisoned themselves within two fences, just like a prison for law-breakers. But they are not in jail yet! May that prison not end them in hell for their part in poor leadership.

There are two places we go when we break the law. Whether it is jail or hell, it is hard to see through to the light of freedom from either place. For some, it is a life sentence. Once it is given, we can serve it forever. Yet, there are those who live life free of others in a prison of living in this divide too. We see them on our streets everywhere with no job or a job at the top alone. No pride or so much pride that they become blinded. No home or an exquisite mansion with no one at their door. We can be lost at either level because we are separated by our own ignorance.

The fence has closed in on them. They believe they are less or more and no longer wish to be any other way. They believe what the other says can be true about them because of their color in the divide, whether that is lowly or supreme. As a so-labeled White, I am encouraged by societal projections to believe I can become so many horrible things history has revealed from that group's past. However, I cannot fit that mold and choose not to.

I could have joined any of the White supremacist groups currently standing. Let's face it: there are many more than I wish to speak of, and these groups are people from our lowest parts of society to the very top of it too. Of course, the leaders in these groups are the ones guilty of leading us wrongly. Just as much as it is our responsibility for taking part in it.

The fences on color are coming down very slowly, and if I were going to pick where I see it breaking down first, it is the so-called Whites in the middle classes. How can anyone actually have pride in the past mistakes of so many in that group? Perhaps that is one of the primary reasons I want no part in it. Although I do not even see our likeness in these colors at all.

I must say I do appreciate some other changes coming now in this evolving future about what we should ban in our society. However, we are still attacking a past with banning children's books thinking that will help the future—perhaps. But I think not.

If we were to ban reading, music, games, groups, or whatever, the problems surrounding our ignorance will evolve and rear their ugly heads in the future. Look at what is boldly beating us in the face and ears every day. The thing about our children not learning the wrong thing is not in the books of our past. It is in the rhythm and beats in our streets, radios, and other media today. Yesterday is gone, and thank God it is not lost.

Today, slang and deprecating terms seem to be supported, if not celebrated. More and more, I find myself hearing "White Trash" used by artists, similar to hip-hop artists using the n-word. If it is COOL or TRENDING to build one color up and the other down, then racism has support again and again. Only building the fences higher and higher again.

One of the saddest parts of this whole color divide is that out of the four colors, two will remain the longest because both have been losing their heritage more and more each day. In other words, losing their ethnicity.

I have found many so-called Whites here in the South who no longer know their ethnicity, nor the native language of their forefathers. As far as the mindset of these people, if you live here, you speak as we do. Their ethnicity has been bred out.

And so it was for the slaves in our country too. Their own ethnicity was bred and bled out over time. They have lost their heritage with it, along the way to becoming Americans. Hence, we made them Americans one generation after the next, only to become natives of our nation without the right to be that native.

What is even sadder is our so-called Black population was captured by mostly different tribes of their own countrymen and sold as slaves to trade for new worldly possessions. These poor folks were taken from places where they did not know their own written language due to the fact that there was no need for it in their own culture back then. Their entire culture has been lost to them forever thanks to racism. They were the spoils of war and its False Color Divide.

Freedom was taken from them by their own desire for possessions to better their lives and ruin their own countrymen by sending them off to faraway lands. So now stands a color of people in racism as African when all Africans are not just African. Some are Egyptian, Algerian, Nigerian, and so forth.

The same goes for those who are White too. There are many generations of them who have ancestors exiled by kings to our land also, with the same dilemma of not knowing their ethnicities any longer due to their multiple generations of nativity here in the United States. Ethnicities are being erad- icated by a social disease called racism for false color instead.

No matter what can divide us beings, we will find ways to be part of one thing or another. There will always be new leaders who will build fences to try to keep us in or out, which is what they were taught to do by their predecessors. This also puts those in parties, very much like politics, only to corral us into their perspective. They know how to influence our leaders in leading us straight into their fences. The powers that be need us to continue electing desired leadership, so they act as if they are with us.

An example is the Democratic Party. That party was once racially against our African American population. They had their fences so high that they did everything they could to stop them from voting in their areas of office. They were successful in doing so for hundreds of years in this country. Until they began to lose ground to the Republican Party, who had almost all the Black vote then. The first Black man in public office was Republican. His name was Hiram Rhodes Revels.

Fences change for many reasons. We can only pray that it will end one day. Maybe when more of us finally see that the idea or politics of it is completely wrong and damaging to us all.

We will continue down this road as long as we allow those who lead us there. Like those who were storming our Capitol with racial supremacy and every racial riot we have had in our dark past. It will continue as long as we continue this way too.

Perhaps we need a new march upon the world and America. One that ends it for those who are willing to take part. Tear down your fence! There is no reason for being part of a lie in the false colors of Black or White when there is only one race. We live together, work together, and learn together. Anyone dividing us by color is racist. Whether it is a single being or whole governments, they continue racism within our world.

Be INDIVISIBLE, with no fence that divides humankind. Allow only God to choose our heaven or hell alone as our judge for our spiritual future.

4

JUSTU, JUSTUS, OR IS IT JUSTICE?

Justu

I have been many places here and abroad. I have been in many situations I wanted to be in and some I wish I had never been in. I have made a lot of mistakes, some simple and some very close to ruining my life and its freedom. I have felt the weight of my transgressions and the weight of those put upon me too. I have put myself first only to make myself feel I should have thought to be last. I must say I have learned a lot and still am learning more and more each day.

I must give the greatest teacher in my life, God through Jesus, the greatest support of all. Thank you, Lord and Savior, to whom I honestly owe my life and support in return. Without Him, my life, as many of us have found out already, could be still a living hell. He is one of the main reasons I am writing this now in my life.

The idea of "Justu" (just you) is an idea that we all go through. We grow up learning all we do only to grow to some chance of adulthood, with the right to do anything and everything we think we may wish or want to do. Hence the "Justu" as being finally our own responsibility.

But that really is not what we become after all. We have been molded by our learning experiences, which when it comes to racist ideas of the past mixed with our own ideas, gets really fuzzy. I can only imagine the views that others can have, but I certainly have drawn my own over time.

For one thing, the idea of me being a so-called White never fit for me and never will. In history, it was always about people in some sort of place in life that I have never been able to relate to. I am not a person of wealth or entitlement. My education is not mastered in any collegiate form. I did start to go to college late in life, only to resign due to health changes in my fifties. I am not political as to pick a side from the main two, Democratic or Republican.

When it comes to the idea of picking to be part of the racist forms of race, whatever they can be, I would never choose one. I will never be part of a religious group or congregation that separates any of us. Nor will I accept someone telling me God says in His words to be another race other than the one He already created: human.

In the words I know to be God's words, we are in His image, not ours. No other living life on our planet is divided by the idea of race because there is only one Human Race made by God alone, not humankind, just as there is only one animal kingdom.

If you think nature made us by evolution, keep in mind that nature itself cannot confirm this. Adopting these theories of origin religiously has led to racist theories about our species—such as eugenics. And we are the greatest fools to follow these ideas at face value, without question, to date. Furthermore, making each "Justu" responsible for our own decisions in this lie of color and False Color Divide. So to the "Justu," wake up and look at yourself in the mirror as we do by grooming ourselves to face the day ahead. Just look into the mirror, as Michael Jackson once wrote so well, and change to groom yourself again to the truth you see.

Each and every one of us are in the image of a human being who is uniquely different from another because you're as individual as God. So please be yourself, without false concepts. He never told us through scripture that we are exactly as Him; He told us we are in His image.

Another unique difference in every one of us is our DNA. However, it is not by racial difference at all because that kind of DNA does not exist. But it is true that you can place many of us to origins even more detailed to where our ancestors came from around the entire world.

Science is designed to take all problems apart to find the answers of the unknown. It is also true that some answers have only seemed true until another person discovered pivotal information that alters what was once considered fact. That "fact" of racial division still does not exist; only the lie continues.

But what is more true is we all have our own unique DNA that makes us all singular as humans beings in God's image. He made us all different from one another, yet all one Human Race.

If you were to really want to possibly know a color, you could go to a paint store. Then have the person who mixes paint scan your skin to try and reproduce your uniquely different color if you wish. I would bet it will not exactly fit to any of the false colors humankind or time has made us.

Plus, your skin tone is different in different places upon your body. So, if you don't like the first choice, choose a different spot on yourself to match your personalized view of yourself, but do not do this to others, please.

Racism is choosing to be a false color by choice. In the beginning of racism was the idea that the White race had some sort of greater level of intelligence, power, greatness, or rights of being on top. However, that is torn down every single day by those in whom God and their own will have proven the theory be absolutely false.

Justus

Now is this "Justus" (just us) thing the same as politics? Well, when it comes to this False Color Divide, it can also be the parties of color in racism too. Of course it is, so if I believe I am any one of the false colors because I want to be part of that group, am I a racist? Yes, by action and fact, that is what I will have chosen and will teach the next person who believes me and follows in my footsteps. The next person is adding the numbers to my Justus platform.

Well, whether you are in any of these so-called races, you are being led to being a part of a race by racism. You are being led and you have decided to follow someone else's ideals and beliefs without even giving yourself a right to decide who you are. Certainly not yourself, so you are now part of the Justus.

People have guided us, and we still fall in line over the same bullshit every time if we are party to it. By doing so, we also become very political, no different than we do with political parties fighting for a seat in government.

We listen to our party tell us what is, by their own and their party's view, wrong with the other side's thinking or doings. Whether it is fact or not, we are party to it, we accept it and then move forward, repeating it even if it is wrong. Racism is very much the same type of party.

Quite frankly, I hope and wish for you to be greater than the possible gratitude you may feel belonging to any such thing. We all need to discover what helps us find our individuality, but it never should rely on the idea of creating oppositions that will trouble us on life's journey. Life really is short, and our aim to please should move in directions that build bridges, not block them.

I am glad overall that the idea of WHITE SUPREMACY is almost dead with most so-called Whites today. Very rightfully so. Because most of us do not think highly of the idea of it anymore at all. Plus, we should note most people do not consider themselves to be in a supreme state of being over others.

Now the United States is most certainly still evolving when it comes to racism. Native Americans continue to refer to themselves by specific tribes and ancestry—they have yet to adopt or encompass that history as a RED race, and I do not think they ever will. They have their own lives in the "Justus" streams of thinking, and it is not in the idea of competition with other races at all. Their times of war and conflict are over, and they wish to live in peace and harmony the rest of their lives as long as they can among us. They have accepted that conflict has no value.

Now the so-called platform of being BLACK has certainly evolved over these past couple of hundred years. They have come a long way being called BLACK. They have also recreated a platform of "Justuses," which has become great in many ways for many wonderful reasons.

They have had great leaders who lead with God, getting them rights they deserved from the beginning. We are all rightfully deserving of the same equal rights.

In sports, they have become some of the greatest athletes in competition, breaking all sorts of records all the time. In the NFL right now, they are taking their platform to raising awareness to the wrongs in our society in our streets, with a main focus on police and governing approaches to dealing with these problems everywhere across America. No one can blame them for it either. Our government's past has been wrong since the beginnings of our history about the way to govern humankind overall.

There are now many NFL players who are so-called biracial, leading the way to trying to end and fight racist ideals by boldly standing for us all. Not just on one side but standing for all humans to be united by ending racism in the game and on our streets today. However, their actions sadly fall short of accomplishing an ever evolving goal. There is too much pride still, and too many people believing the lie of False Colors. Furthermore, division surrounding "biracial" doesn't appear to help the mission on any level.

Allow me to add your attention to a matter of importance about the so-called biracial beings on our planet. First and foremost, these citizens receive some of the population's greatest disrespect and dishonor over being biracial. How so? some may ask.

Well, number one, their parents are given unequal respect in the manner that only one parent's race is allowed for their child. Racism works against one from the other every time. It seems in every case for the Black and White child, they are forced by racism to be Black.

Why? Because of racism! Across the spectrum of False Colors, alike supports alike and rejects anything considered mixed. White culture rejects children of mixed background. Black culture rejects them just the same. As do Brown, Red, and Yellow. In fact, a spectrum of entirely new words emerges as people left in between seek strength in identity. Each society has its problems with the mixing of different ethnicities. This is unfortunately consistent across the globe. The "Justus" platform perpetuates everywhere thanks to any given leadership one may follow.

I'm BLACK and I'm proud. I'm White and why shouldn't I be still proud? Well, they may be absolutely right to be proud, but it is still absolutely wrong to be either if it is to end one day. We should be proud of our own being, not a group who all too often makes another group shine less every time.

Both sides have their wrongs and rights. But because they won't join the Human Race to be one, it will take longer for change, not just in the United States but also across the globe. It will take the individual approach to make the change one by one. It will be many more years until each of us can shed the False Color Divide. Damn the divide; it is our culture now. The only Justuses continue segregation of our world by groups. Which means, in racism, we are these false colors.

Justice

Isn't that what we have? Well, do we? Many of us continue to argue that very thing in the courts, not only in our country but also in other places around the world. We know that to be true just here in the United States every time there is an election. It becomes the very thing that leaders try to lead our voters to the polls with all the time. We need justice!

The year 2020 was a highlight in history with supremacy playing a part on two different levels of stature and race. Politics had its glory one way or another, and as far as the Republicans' side, they had their renewed bout with WHITE supremacy interfering with their losses.

The Republican Party has had a history of the opposing side labeling them as racist and the supremacy side for many years. Probably because the party has mostly been guided by the rich of our country who have paid and lobbied for the Republican Party's campaigns and support for many of these years as well. Most of these supporters are considered to be White. Although in the past it was the Democrats who were racist—or are they really still racist, and they've just convinced you they are not?

President Donald J. Trump did not help but showed he wouldn't voice malice against White supremacy groups in 2019. Was it because he is a racist? One would think that, of course, but I think it was more that he is far too susceptible to the idea that he is superior in strategy and management. It fills his head with dumb ideas like worrying over the idea of losing votes he thought he needed to win.

He was not the master of the game on this at all, and he proved so by losing an election that mattered to many Americans. His loss was not just his own. It was also the loss of what many considered a necessary change— stopping the opposing party from selling out their country and overspending the nation's resources.

Politicians also abuse their campaign funds. They make sure they spend all they can instead of using funds to help our country one way or another. Gluttony is a sin, where campaign funds allow campaigners to fill their belly in abundance.

So, will there be justice now that a different party is in power? Only if we continue to fight for change while the new politicians are in office. They will guide themselves more toward their own ideals rather than our country's. Their ideals will be to receive as much as they can along the way to honor what they need before honoring what we need as a country as a whole.

This country needs its unity again in the world's eyes and our own. We are looked upon as if our unity is truly false more than anywhere in the world because of our racism. Our people trouble over a racial divide and its differences before troubling over our medical system, schooling, or ways to lift up our society by healing our social problems.

Crime continues rising because there is no way for many to survive past their mistakes that lead them to doing it again and again. The idea of a Department of Corrections never corrects or leads a criminal away from crime.

So, what does society have for this? Nothing but a cell. We are letting convicts continue to be what we can put away. Instead, we accept the idea that one day we can put them away forever once they commit enough crimes. So now society can foot the bill for each and every one in prison instead of steering them back to being a productive part of our society.

That may be justice in some way; however, it is not in another way, because politicians commit crimes in government and almost always get away with it. This only shows that government alone is its own "Justus" in our society overall, meaning there is no justice overall. Is there?

This is ridiculous. As the saying goes, Teach a man to fish and he will have food not only for himself but also for his family and maybe even further still for his community as well. Then once he can, he will no longer have a need to commit crime again. He will also have a sense of pride of doing well before his peers, which will encourage him to teach others along the way like his sons, daughters, family, and community, thereby breaking the chains of crime in his family and ours.

The United States, just like third-world countries, now has its problems where families are led to crime. Crime in urban cities has many so-called Black, White, and other ethnic groups fall to family-led crime teachings because of the norms of how we live in poverty. I know this because I was led in this way, and I led as well in this manner before. Justice begins with honesty, so I must be honest too.

I thank God my family is doing well and for the most part has been led away from this mindset thanks to God, and I can only hope in small part from my own doing. I'd rather give all my thanks to God.

Having God lead us is good for us because His law is much stricter in one way. He also has a better support for forgiveness for those who follow than we do.

But humankind's law has many loopholes. Look at alcohol, drugs, and sex. Loopholes by law exist for many reasons, but the major reason for it is desire and capitalism. They are the hand of humankind—not God-kind. Many of us need God's help to overcome these obstacles in our lives. I know I am thankful He has been there with me; I also pray He may be there for many others.

Being repressed by racism is a driving force that helps lead us the wrong way all too often. Lift a being beyond their repression and you lift them to succeed. Take away racism by law and you give a way to stand taller than a party can. Most of us have only two legs to stand on; however, our government is meant to help support each of us through justice to strengthen our legs, not take them out from under us.

If law did not allow or have within it the idea that there is more than one Race, it would be the beginning of the onset of ending racism by law second and only second. The truth is that we must be the first to change the laws. This of course will take time, but it would lead us by law to a truer equality than we have had to date by law alone, thereby giving our Human Race the justice it deserves overall in this country and perhaps many others.

Special Note

> POLITICS: the activities associated with the governance of a country or other areas [or, "RACES,"] especially the debate or conflict among individuals or parties having or hoping to achieve power.

When I found how Dictionary.com defines *politics* on my phone, I could not help but insert "races" for obvious reasons. Sound familiar? There will always be those who will guide you to believing in a need for them to achieve power with your help. But that can only be done when you let them do so.

Look at the outcome of our last election of 2020. The price of gas increased up to $5 per gallon in California, while here in Florida, it was below $2 per gallon before the election. All within six months' time, it has reached above $3 per gallon. Lumber has gone up threefold and even four times as much in the same time. Across the board, all commodities have gone up beyond reason.

The worst of it was our "wonderful" leaders led a campaign using racism to elevate their platform by using it to lead so-called Blacks their way and then taking all those against racism along with them too. When it comes to power-hungry leaders, we will be used every single time for their own goals, not yours or your family's.

Of course, the crime of price gouging is happening this very moment, but you will more than likely not hear about that till the next election. In the end, no one in government will be charged with a crime; only slander will happen.

Also, we will hear about how the poor can no longer afford to own a home or repair the ones they so desperately are trying to maintain. Or about how many families live on the streets of the United States due to inflation, all from the results of the 2020 elections' winners.

Remember, part of the excuses for this will be the raise in wages as the result of the 2020 election outcome. Or that it is also the backlash of import tariffs from the last man in office. Their way of justice is to turn the blame without ever repairing the damage done.

They're the winners, and we are their devoted losers who now fall victim with the rest of our country, along with them too. All thanks to our beloved leaders, the liars who lead us wrongly! That is the JUST to those facts of politics we can follow blindly by being deaf to what we hear.

We are not a color we are not, nor can you raise a wage without increasing costs across the whole spectrum within the economy. We reap what they sow. Their bullshit becomes ours by our own voting in their will for us, if that is what you really believe they are doing. We get the proverbial curveball of justice that heads straight home to their plate while missing our own entirely.

5

QUESTION RACE

The idea of multiple races is a very questionable concept that we all should look at. If racism was created by humankind approximately five centuries ago, should we not look at it again now so many years later? Of course we should, especially now.

The concept somehow lives on today as a trophy to some of us, which is understandable given how much some people have endured to get to where they stand now. Although not all have had to endure as much as many have, nor do we deserve any hailing for their endurance neither.

Then on the ignorance side of it, where do we have a right to stand in a show of hate toward another, as racism can do? This platform has turned our society into turmoil for hundreds of years. And before the racism part, another couple of thousand years were spent in the turmoil of war because conquerors aimed to be supreme over others. Hate is a power that corrupts, hence racism and its origin.

So, if we are created by God or through natural evolution on our planet, how does that give the right to humans to make a choice of division by race? It certainly does not, especially when science has no support for the concept. Or are you the conquered who has lost your individuality to the conqueror's victory, as you fall in line with this False Race put upon you?

The people who formed this concept had their own reasoning and agenda for it, and you can almost lay down bets to their reasoning being used to be hateful one way or another about others. You can also bet it was to state how much more intelligent or wise they were in comparison.

They were the leaders back then who stood on their powers in their glory, without giving glory to others. Their sacrifice was others; their own pawns even fell before they did. Plus, back then it was off with our heads if we tried to argue against them, even if we were their own acclaimed race.

Today, it may be more civilized without the barbaric tools of the past. However, the world today is still very barbaric. Especially when someone in the honored position of law enforcement goes beyond their duty to act much more in their own interest. This officer should be a respected enforcer of our laws and never take the law into their own hands.

Referring to all the officers who do not take the law into their own hands, we should always give them the respect they deserve for doing a job that many of us could not do so well. Thank you all for your service to our country as a whole.

Yet look, we are separated races, which means we will always be in competition with or against one another. It is hard to tell the difference anymore. Because as they try to say, there are two sides to a coin. However, that is wrong too. There are two flat sides and then there is a side that encircles the two different sides, is there not?

In the United States, the legal idea of race as written in law has a very unclear definition. I will explain how. As it is known, we somehow have four types of races in the world: the RED, the BLACK, the WHITE, and the YELLOW. But this is not really the case in the United States for many reasons.

The RED race would be American Indians. These once very poor natives to America do not consider themselves to be this hate term or type of race at all. Only those who changed their lives with the racism they brought with them from Europe call them that. So, the RED race is not what our laws pertain to today.

Then there is the YELLOW race. I cannot tell you its exact origin. But it is to symbolize the Asian origins of people from that region. I also cannot understand why they would consider themselves to be this color either. They are not Yellow in any way at all. Also, the few Asian people I have talked to about this find it absolutely ridiculous.

Now in the era of Social Darwinism in the late nineteenth and early twentieth centuries, race groups were placed as evolving in unparalleled lines on one playing field, with "Whites" overtaking "Blacks," "Reds," and "Yellows."

I remember coming across a few old sentiments in which White overtakes the ladder as if superior in some way. It does so in a racist form because that was the way of thinking by those of European origin then, and also by Charles Darwin and his theory of evolution. He also once presented a fifth race that is not often thought of by people as being a race until today: "BROWN." Quite frankly, this is the only one that actually comes close to being true. Perhaps that is why they dropped it from their race descriptions stemming from European theories.

So, America's most influential evolution came with the migration of Europeans who brought with them this Darwinian mindset to our culture. With it came a human-made division of races that Americans have toiled over since our colonization. By the idea of races in American law, it never states the FIVE colors of Darwinism, nor does it state the most known colors of division from our past—of the four false colors of division. Plus, in the recent years, it feels as though American media only really considers the two colors of Black or White as racial differences or divides.

A race should only be what we choose it to be, as in a competition. Being competitive is okay and good for those who wish to compete. Although for those who do, they must compete with an understanding that the victor is the only one who can actually win today; tomorrow comes another and so forth.

In society, there should never be a self-destructive competition between its citizens. That is what RACISM is! So, if we hail from one color or another, we split our society in the wrong manner. To stand in this manner, whether it is WHITE or BLACK, you stand against us all as a whole ever existing.

In school growing up, most of us were made to recite a pledge each and every day that began back around World War I, called the PLEDGE OF

ALLEGIANCE. In remembering that pledge, I can remember more than once the mistakes I heard from other students saying it wrong, and this has proved to still be true today. Many of us have made ourselves individuals before "INDIVISIBLE."

What I mean by that is many students only said the pledge as they understood it, and many misunderstood the word "indivisible" as being "individual" instead.

Yes, we are all very much individual and should be very proud to be as we are. There is no rightful reason for that to vary from one person to another.

Nevertheless, our teachers did a very poor job of teaching the meaning of the indivisible part of our pledge. Perhaps the redundancy of having to recite it every day made it mean less to them. However, that very pledge brought a nation together in hard times to achieve the impossible.

I am here to tell all who opposed or stand against our pledge stand also against our communities who are still having trouble with our false racial divide. The NFL and the assault on our Capitol are prime examples of how divisible we have become.

We are but one nation but divided by racism. We are divisible by our law as well because it allows us to divide our humankind. Not just in the United States, but also around the world, racism has divided our humanity with no proof other than the tales of once-believed liars who believed even their own tales.

6

LIVING THE LIE

I know that for many of us, it is hard to lie. As demonstrated by statistics, U.S. citizens are a massive group of believers in God. We are a multitude of nationalities with a variety of religious beliefs all mixed together into one huge melting pot.

Because of this, one would think there are many fewer liars in our society. Add to that the element of being all together under God, as we have pledged in our national Pledge of Allegiance.

Then on top of that, we are all attached to some form of obligation where the foundation is to always be honest. Families are the basic place we hold trust that we will not be misled. But this is one of the major places it all turns to changing our lives.

Too many of us grow up living in the lie of racism. Remember racism is over 500 years old, and it has been passed down from one generation to another. Which means that it has been passed down by our parents and every other influence around us throughout our growing years. It was being passed down in my home once upon a time too.

So, we grew up in racism, and all too many of us are taught the lies of racism to this very moment in our lives. How does that make you feel? Can you think of any lies that you were taught? Does it stir up a feeling that makes you believe those lies? Do you at times think of another as if they are so different that racism fits the moment? Can you be influenced to say what you never would wish to be said about you? Or wait, you say these things because you actually believe they can never be you! All too often these questions fit somehow. Why? Because we live in the racist lie around us.

Well, it does happen almost everywhere now. It happens on every side of the fence that we make around us. Our past learning experiences emerge, and oops there it is, all too often. I have made these mistakes in my younger years; I can honestly admit it. I have learned from my mistakes against others as well as the mistakes that were made against me.

Remember, in racism we are on a fence with our false issues. What is used most of the time is that we are made to be in a stereotypical image within the lies of racism. Or even worse, the bad mistakes of others' past deeds. The stereotypes do not represent the person in front of you most of the time.

Racist lies make nothing true. Yet these false truths are making even more lies upon lies, very progressively and in a way that is certainly hard to change. It is pretty confusing for those growing up around us. How are you handling the lies told to you? Are you telling others you're RED, BLACK, WHITE, or YELLOW? Are you stuck living in the lie?

If you are, please try your best to change the past and be honest with those who trust you. Stand next to them in a mirror and admire one another for who each of you are beside each other. Hold up the colors of racism with you both standing there together.

This is your chance to be honest and explain what these colors have stood for in our society for hundreds of years. You can change the course of other people's futures with yours alongside one another. We are not these colors, but we are exactly as we see ourselves. Our own family is uniquely made in God's image, not humankind's.

This Sunday, I am going to a church that I attended for the first time last week. I thoroughly enjoyed it. However, I would like it even more if God helps them to find their way back to what we all are too. His image alone, not humankind's.

I hope and pray in the near future to tell you the change really is happening in this church and in many others soon as well. God has never shown His will to be racist; why should we do this as His children? If we are stewards of His teachings, it is our job to teach the same in our church weekly where we can.

I must say that I have never heard any leader of the churches that I have attended mention the lies about racism or whether there was any truth to us being any of these false colors. However, I have heard that it takes place in churches I have neither seen nor witnessed in person or on TV.

On the unfortunate side of hearing preaching from people who are considered Black, I have heard mention of the racial divide. Of course, I am old enough to understand why it was said in the first place. I also understand that its origin at each occurrence was stirred up by altercations from some so-called opposing racist side of bad intentions in what these preachers considered to be against their own.

This is racist just as much as it was racist for the other side to create a moment that the preacher had to talk about in their sermon. There stood a man of God condemning a racist action by separating the people of his church as a race other than what God made.

I am very sure if I search for a church in the White Supremacy realm, I could still find a preacher making the very same mistakes. Even today, still in their own place of worship too. There was once a past in our country where it happened all too often and created hate groups like the Ku Klux Klan.

Lies are being told, and lies will always be told, about others. But remember, be the devil and you will live in the devil's lies too, meaning if you wish to be something of false origin and give false witness as truth, you are the liar that racism supports.

So it has become with the assault upon our Capitol. Its origin was a political divide and a belief that there was voting tampering, where President Trump led those who were there to come first that day due to undocumented voting disputes.

But some of those attending also turned it into a racial dispute on top of that. The racist in the midst of the whole group made all who attended guilty of racism when all were not. This gave the false idea that the Republican

Party could appear possibly racist when it truly as a whole is not. See how that kind of behavior can reflect on others who have no part in what's done around them?

It's called guilt by association, even if it is not true. That has been the whole start of racism since its conception. One lie upon another, building gaps to set us apart from one another. Racism is a really sharp tool used against us all and has left many scars along the way, socially and politically.

We are supposedly one great nation that has been heralded in our past and present as being under God. Yet we still stand apart in the social divide of racism all too often. In the NFL, a slogan is written on the backs of many helmets that reads, "It takes all of us." Why? Because it is true. Why else were we made to be together under God's plan?

There are many of us who seek counsel with our Lord. The name of our Lord may differ from one belief to another; however, most of us will agree that there is only one God over us all. We are all similar in a need for quiet times in prayer to sort out our reasoning with Him and with ourselves in our own ways.

How do you question Him and yourself in prayer? Do you speak to Him in the sense of your views of dividing yourself from others? Probably not, because deep within the mess of our social divide, we never try that kind of talk with God. At least most of us, I pray.

There is a really good reason for that, and you know what that answer is, don't you? We are not made to be in heaven with these social divides at all. Because right there inside your soul that was also created by God, you know He did not create the lies of racism; humankind did. If racism still lingers inside your own being, you also know you are against God's own creation. Racism is ruling you more than God Himself over any reason you may have.

We certainly need reasons to change, which can be found in the many mistakes we inevitably make over the course of our lives. Our lies are probably one of the most important things we can forget we have made over time. Remember the truth about lies. A liar does not always remember their own lies, and that is how they are caught almost every time.

The internet is full of lies, and if you look hard enough, you can find them in so many places. I for one like to catch those who try to invite themselves on my Facebook as ladies who are looking for friendship with men to lure them into believing they are real. I can always catch them because they are lying. Do I do it to find another to be with? Not at all. I have someone, and quite frankly, I am also very tired of being friend requested by liars looking to take advantage of others.

Now in my life, I question many as to what they say and wonder if they are honest too often. I know this is wrong of me; a fault that life has carved into me after too many lies. Racism, politics, media, and relationships have shown me to question the value of their honesty.

But it teaches me a truth overall. There is a need for many to survive. Is survival always led by truth? I think not. Many times, people find their own way to a solution, and all too often, it is by misleading and glorifying themselves before you. This is one reason racism began. It was a glorification of the ones who led it.

Thank God always that He is not them, but He will be strict when the time comes for you to be honest.

We cannot as humans fathom the thoughts of our God. However, put yourself as being in His shoes before you continue living in the lie. Lies are best at finding more lies. The truth never needs to find cover from anything.

7

THE POWER OF RACISM

Be honest—is there some kind of idea somewhere that a racist power has value anymore? Does being a color to join in a union with others really help or serve your needs? Help us all to understand if you can, as a good leader, show a value to everyone in this color you continue to believe we should be.

If I am to be led by you to believe there is value in your narration, what can you assure me in the end? Nothing overall, as the record shows from past influences. Sure, it is very uplifting to have someone lift our spirits. Although if it is for only the moment you speak to me, and its true value disappears a short time after the inspiration, what then did it really do?

It is very much the same as what Norman Whitfield and Barrett Strong wrote in their song "War." Conflict is good for absolutely nothing. We only use these types of values to divide people, not join them. This should also show those of us who are believers in the idea of going to a heavenly place to wake the hell up and smell the crap we are being sold here on earth.

The "powers" that stem from hate are not for you to be happy at all. They are the powers of ill will to further distance one side from another. They aim to give a leader the will to rule over most of us who are in the groups they can take power over.

There is no government or platform here on earth to care for all of us. We are divided every which way. Whether it is a country or political organization of some sort. They are there to be your leader, with you footing their bills before your own. Render what you must, but do not render your soul.

I will say that as long as we divide ourselves by color, we will suffer the wake we deserve from its wave. Sure, many will always survive, and the reason for that is the game is meant to last as long as you will play.

George Floyd suffered by asphyxia and then death thanks to racism, as have many others. Just because there is some shaded color difference between us, there is no reason to follow the racist ideas that someone should be treated wrongly because of their color. Nor is there a reason we should fear another based upon their possible ethnic differences, or the way they act when accused of committing a crime either.

Those who are in power or who have power in our lives must become a greater influence for change. It really is in our power as individuals to begin the change toward humanity's unity first. Any reason for division should be based only on reasons of not wishing to be close with another because of personal preferences. Not because of the narrow perspective of racism that makes many others the same likeness.

Racism's power is the same as a car. It needs fuel, and where you get your fuel is as important as it is how it helps your car run. There are many places you can get fuel, but the best fuel is one that keeps you from having problems with your car.

Racism's power is a fight no one ever needs to be involved in. Each and every one of us is altogether worthy of being in the same place and time. Let no leader separate you from your fellow citizens or world again. Racism is only powered by its pawns. As a pawn in racism, your fueling abilities can keep it running beyond understanding.

There is some irony that chessboards are black and white. There is also some irony that certain leaders play their subjects against one another.

Finally, knowing that humankind really has no provable separate races is a game changer. What is it they say when a chess game is won? "Checkmate." Game over!

Racism loses, as it always has done since it began. Racism has never joined a nation, nor can it ever give our world peace.

8

HOW ARE YOU LEADING?

So, leadership may be the last thing you think to do. You may just be that individual soul who goes through their own life never wanting any part of leadership at all. However, by doing just that, you are leading others around you every single day without ever looking behind you.

I can assure you that someone is watching because I've watched everyone around me on a daily basis. So is the way of most of us. The way we carry ourselves inspires someone up or down. On the upside, we can find ourselves inspired by ideas that may lead us to leading others. On the downside, we never consider it affecting another person, although it can.

I have lived poorly at times with my own depression, and I have done my best to live with my depression too. Some of my depression is about racial issues that pertain to a future for my daughter and her sons, who are called biracial today. I worried about what will inspire them one day, no different than remembering something in the past that inspired me up or down.

I am living with my depression as I write this to you this very minute. Is it easy? Hell, no! But the last place I ever wish be again is down and out. It is a choice when you can see that you have one.

Depression is not something every one of us can escape. I also know there are times when we are not able to see our road ahead. Nor may we be able to step forward at these moments in our lives. Although when there is only one way to go from down, that is when it is time to look up.

For me my up is a twofold leadership skill developed by past experiences with up and down. God has been there as my silent counsel every step of the way. Did I know that? Of course not. I was brought to church as a young man of around ten years old.

Did I believe God really existed then? No, I did not; my world was mostly my parents, just like most of us. It takes more than time to have an understanding of God and how He can work for us. Each and every one of us has our very own time and place we get to meet our God. Hopefully you can be that lucky one who, by grace, He accepts before the gates of heaven.

I will say He did inspire me before I knew He was real. I was a loner because I like to wander, think, and watch the world turn around me. While doing this, I sorted out my feelings and those feelings others would teach me as I watched and learned from them too. I also chose to talk to my imagination that God was there listening as my counsel. It was really tough at times, let me tell you.

I matured as my own counsel for way too long, I will tell you that now. We can make many poor decisions as our own counsel. But the upside is we learn a hell of a lot along the way.

One example that stuck out the most for me was I could not look at the world made around me as BLACK and WHITE. This racist thing seemed to drive people into these sides I could not seem to ever pick. Yes, in the late '60s and '70s, there was as much going on about our Racial divides as there is today. There were also too many riots then, just like now.

The riots were a lesson for me to witness concerning their leadership. Our so-called Blacks were being led by leaders who meant well enough in what they thought was right, sure. Just as history repeats itself, so will the people of the future repeat what they have evolved to learn from their past.

So, the people around those leaders then went too far and destroyed millions of dollars of property during each riot, just as they still do now. To date, riots now are destroying billions of dollars of property in our country's communities. But what leaders now and even in the past don't seem to consider is how many of those they lead become first-time criminal offenders.

They were changing their followers' lives, perhaps forever, thanks to their very poor leadership. They also took away these followers' chance to vote for decades, before 2016. Not very smart as a leader who said they were trying to better their lives to make change for their good.

Now this is history even more similar to that of White Supremacy in the American South beginning just after the Civil War. So-called Whites would join together in groups such as the Ku Klux Klan (KKK), wear disguises and white hoods, and burn and vandalize places where they could hurt the Black communities. They were committing crimes that in most cases were not solved nor were people compensated for the damage done. Not much different from today, where crimes still are destroying predominantly Black churches.

Although it is still very much different today. Sure, rioters are wearing hoods to hide their faces while destroying property; however, they are not being led to do it in the same manner as it was done by the KKK. The leaders of the Black movements are not knowingly leading their own to commit these crimes.

Nevertheless, they are fueling the very anger that builds protesters' foolishness into these crimes of hate along the way of each movement. These leaders are antagonizers, who through their speeches, rally their followers to destruction of our communities and sometimes the death of innocent bystanders.

A present-day example just happened in early 2021 while I was writing this. On January 6, at the Capitol Building of the United States of America, thousands of pro-Trump protesters went to protest the November 3 election results. All these protesters were led to believe the election had been somehow rigged. They also believed that was why their candidate, President Trump, had lost the election.

They gathered together at the Ellipse, where their President came to speak before them. He continued to convey his beliefs about what he believed was a rigged election for some two hours of speech. Though there was no conclusive evidence of election fraud, he rallied his citizens to go to the Capitol Building.

Did he actually think they were going to go there to vandalize, break and enter, kill or be killed at our nation's Capitol Building that day? One would only have to wonder, deep down inside, whether he was initially happy with their actions. We would think this to perhaps be true. Of course, days later, he conveyed his disappointment in the protesters' actions. He also conveyed his belief publicly that all who did wrong needed to be brought to justice.

However, he could not admit his wrongdoing as to how he most likely led them to committing their crimes against the Capitol that very day by accident, as so many others in history have led citizens worldwide wrongly to rally against issues of the past. In most cases, the leaders aren't charged, because they never truly tell those they lead to commit these atrocities. No matter how it happened, they were led wrongly by their leader at the time.

There have been successful movements done without this kind of damage in the past. The greatest praise must go to Martin Luther King, Jr., for the personal relationship he had with God and his people at that time he led others. He demanded that they protest peacefully and would always instill pride in his people for the goodwill inside them. He was a great leader of peace and change. He was also an inspiration to me, believing his people were equal to any others on the planet, with us by our sides.

On the other side of the protests where he rallied, there was the local governing police, who failed to act properly, if not legally, especially by today's standards. Martin Luther King's leadership even affected the opposing side over time, but many suffered till they realized how ignorant they had been.

Leadership is not just an act of leading. It should instill in the people it inspires that we are and can be equal to one another. It should in fact somehow lead us to an answer that resolves our complaints without creating more along the way.

Those we lead should never have to fall to the wrongdoings similar to those whom we have complaints about. Never should we lead others to commit crimes against others, nor should the end result be the conviction of those who were led to committing crimes either. That is not leading for good will. It is destroying the value of those who were led to their demise.

History will always convey the sides and their views one way or another at different times. It is also true that history many times only portrays the view of the one who is telling the only side they can see. So, it is important to look further if you wish to know all sides. And it is even more important when in the heat of being led to consider not only both sides but also where you are being led that moment.

Sadly, all this past history to date has not changed the face of racism, even today. So, as you can see, the sides you may pick can lead you today into a Racial divide because the divide still exists. Is that what we really want, or is that what each of us has allowed ourselves to be led by today?

You, before anyone else, know where you wish to be. I cannot lead you to anything your passion is not ready to believe. If you believe you are any single one color, whether a false one or true to yourself, then perhaps you are in your mind as you stand. That is your stand to take. God gave you that absolute right to choose and let no one take it away.

Still, 500 years of people being divided by false terms, issues, and beliefs has turned the world against its own far too long. No politics should ever divide us as a world, let alone a nation as great as ours. We must become the resting place and end to racism once and for all, for our fellow citizens and for the world.

By this point, if you believe anything said in this book, I hope you see the mechanisms behind our division and believe that these colors are false.

A mirror alone can show you your image if you have doubts. Or take some research time to review some facts. That is really much easier on your character than following fools.

I ask you to consider reading this statement as a way to reboot your mindset so that any part of racism that exists within your being can vanish.

I STAND AS AN INDIVIDUAL, AND I AM INDIVISIBLE AND AGAINST RACISM AND THE FALSE COLOR DIVIDE. I AM NOT THESE COLORS, NOR DO I FIT IN A BOX OF CRAYONS FOR OTHERS TO RECOLOR THEIR OWN WAY. ALL HUMANKIND IS ONE RACE TOGETHER, WHICH I AM PART OF AS THE HUMAN RACE AND AS THE ONE AND ONLY ONE RACE UNDER GOD.

9

YOUR COLOR

Without the color of racism, does your color actually diminish? Of course not! As a matter of fact, your color becomes even more defined. Yes, because you gain your own individuality instead. Your so-called false racial group is shed and all its burdens are shed with it too if you finally allow it.

None of us need the burden of outside forces filling our lives because our lives are but our own. Our focus should always first be on what will make us who we wish to become, not what some outside negative force of past generations has wielded down upon us.

To succeed birth alone, we have survived the first challenge of our life. Nevertheless, challenges are what really drive our inner spirits so we can all face the challenges we have each and every day.

Your color is not the outside appearance of some false political arguments set by others. Your color truly is what you make it for yourself. Sure, we cannot dismiss that each and every one of us has a different skin tone. That has set us into being put into groups. However, no group is really what each of us are. We are individuals. Whether our bed is made or not, it should always be done by our own doing.

The best or worst of others does not define us either. Racism does that by its false color platforms. That is why the politics of racism today needs to change. It is those who hail their false colors that keep the momentum of racism going.

Every single character who succeeds does not succeed to glorify the group; they succeed because it is their character's soul accomplishment. Their accomplishments are the color of their character. Not the color of their skin. Their accomplishments are because of their hard work that no one else has done but them alone. That is the color of their character, not some false race.

Character is a person's color. It begins as a child and grows within us. From day one, we learn to react in our life to what is around us. For most of us, it is the smile or a frown that greets us the moment we awaken. More of one or the other is what influences us. It molds how we react to the world around us.

For those who read this from their own negative nature as standard, you need to realize two things. The first is that somewhere in your past, the reactions around you were negative. You accepted it as being how you should look upon our world. It became how you think your own life should be as a standard.

The second nature of negativity would be your outlook on the world around you. If you look upon the world as a gloomy place, all the actions of that world are now by nature dark, unforgiving, and a place of ridicule. This world is not a place where a smile belongs unless it is one of sarcasm.

Sound negative? Sure does! Not an easy place to rise up from and grow a good outlook about the world, its people, or our chances in it. There is no optimism in it at all, and it is a perfect place to breed racism or any other poor belief against others in the world that surrounds us.

This behavior is no color of character that anyone ever truly wants or needs. As a matter of fact, most of us are taught that this is poor character. Nonetheless, the color of this character is unhappiness, and I do not believe it will ever become positive.

A poor judge of character is an artist who paints their world's color against the rest of the background as if they do not fit in. For that artist, they receive exactly what they perceive in return about themselves instead.

Fortunately, for many of us, we have had more smiles than frowns, and the color of these smiles sets us miles apart from a negative outlook in the world. It is those who carry great smiles who see the better and brighter sides in life. They even set their background with the outlook that all is brighter and can be if you wish it to be.

Of course, wishes are not dreams. There is a great difference between the two. Wishes are just a thought of good or bad, and they are not normally pressed upon.

Our dreams are very much different. Dreams, for many of us, become our mission or goal in life. Our world around us was first made from the fabric of dreams. These dreams are building blocks that many of us have accomplished to bring about our changes in and for humankind.

An example of one such dream was a man who was made Black by the world around him. He had a dream and made it a mission in his life in the midst of a world of hate and ignorance around him each and every day. That man even died still labeled by that ignorance and yet that ignorance still thrives today.

However, he worked hard at his dream and made it in many ways a reality. That man was Martin Luther King, Jr., who in a great recorded speech said, "I have a dream!" Is that dream over? Apparently not! Racism still thrives, and men and women are still coined in groups called Black and White. Yet we are still segregated by false races when there is but one Race, humankind.

The point is, he had character far beyond the color he was made. So far beyond his color that it set him up as a character who molded history to make a change that was greatly needed for the time. As it is even still needed today. This also shows his dream has continued even beyond his own life then to ours.

We are our own characters, set into environments that are not always as we may wish or even have dreamed of. Rest assured, we are able to make changes to the color of our character that can change not just our lives but also the lives of others.

Whatever type of leader you may become, may you lead by a color of character that lifts others up and never tears another down. When you see another person down, may the color of your character lift them up with a smile. May it show a person who sees it that your care is for more than just yourself.

And may your smile shine beyond any false color made by others. It may be you who shows them a color of character to become, instead of a color of false care.

As for me, I work to color my soul and being, not the color of my flesh or yours.

10

ANTIRACIST

The thought of being antiracist is great in theory, but it is an even tougher value to have while living among our diverse society as it is now. Most of us cannot imagine what there is to face on just that type of position.

I, for one, am willing to push the envelope to find out what will happen with the opposing side from now on. Because it is the opposing side that needs to change in the future history to come. When I say opposing side, I do not mean a different color; I mean anyone one who wishes to continue arguing to continuing racial views against or for another. Period, point blank.

Remember all the historical facts about White supremacy and its racist past. Which, I am very sorry to say, is not over by a long shot. From the past to the present, the coin certainly is conveyed to show heads or tails—but we often forget about the circumference side.

Also, major media coverage today has had a greater impact than we realize overall. In truth, each type of life matters, but these lives should not still be divided because it still festers racism, not any type of antiracism.

Well, it is easy for those of us who hold firmly to a position without resistance. But when faced with the resistance of the opposing side, will you stand down and say you still are antiracist?

Here is the problem for many, and the police are included in this. We can believe we are antiracist in most situations, but then a conflict occurs with what is considered the opposing race. The matter gets out of hand when the opposition reacts in a threatening way, then fear or hate takes root. Every situation, of course, can be different in many ways.

Of course, average citizens have a greater fear than an officer who carries a gun. Conflict in the streets today is always considered a possible deadly moment as the news depicts almost daily in so many places. But the situation has been cultivated over hundreds of years of fear and hate on both sides, where the results of these types of conflicts have made us so leery or make assumptions as to what can happen.

Can you still be antiracist as it happens, or even once you get to leave the situation afterward? I believe for most of us, we would have great difficulty doing so. Why? Because of our learned behaviors after so many years of bad politics passed down by European trends before us and still continuing today.

Politics are the guiding force, whether it is by kings, governments, communities, or families. We have governed ourselves almost beyond repair. Yet still there are only a few who are trying their best to be godly in the manner of God's leadership. God has guided us on the matter of humankind's reactions and how our reactions to the world should be. We should praise those who try to be antiracist where they can daily. Especially when it is still hard for many.

It is a wonder how police officers can do their job, as hard it may be with racism added. Their job is in part to be antiracist in their daily tours of duty. It took hundreds of years for the darkest-skinned people of our societies to overcome violence, oppression, hatred, and racism to stand up and take the abuse they have until now.

A law enforcement officer has a full hand to play every day. For one, they must face people who fear them and whom they fear also. The officer faces, all too often, an opposition guided by false assumptions about the attitudes of law enforcement on race. Then there is the perspective of any person questioned during the investigation. When anyone's reaction reflects the racism found between one party and the other, the situation turns inside out and departs from the actual purpose of the investigation. It turns into a matter of foolish pride, yes, but it is also how we evolve after so many years of being put down. We become defiant.

Now they won't even stand down when face to face with a gun threatening them, even when in the hands of a police officer with a gun who is afraid. It amazes me, but also it does not. I, too, can be guilty of being daring when faced with the threat of a gun. In fact, I have done this on more than one occasion.

You can't run from a gun when it is aimed at you. Nor can we run like the superhero The Flash to beat a bullet. Fear can stop most of us when faced with it, but some of us are just too damn pissed off when threatened by one too.

The group that will have the hardest time overcoming racism will be law enforcement because they are the ones who face it today more than any other citizen. They are on the front line to stop racism from destroying and harming innocent citizens in our communities.

It is most important for us who believe we are trying to be antiracist to lobby to change law enforcement—which can only be changed through the law itself.

By doing so, we can be the catalyst of change and the chain reaction against racism that may lead us to ending this once and for all.

Purpose

What does the idea of being antiracist mean to you? Is there purpose in it for you? What will it change in your life if you really try to live that way?

Peace is a purpose that many of us should desire. Would it help you or your family to have more peace if racism was not around you? There are still many places around us where the element of racism crosses our path.

Growing up, peace in my home was disrupted by the news at times. It influences a household by portraying a view that can be turned into thoughts that did—and can—stir up the mind toward racism if you let it. My parents led me there when they saw what they had seen on television at those times. Did they mean to lead me wrong? No, of course not.

Did I go beyond my home growing up and have my experiences with what they taught me on the streets in my life? Sorry to say that I did, and it taught me I was damn wrong. I'm even more proud to say that it did that. I cannot be proud of racism; not me. I have just seen way too much of it over the years. There has been more than sixty years of life around me so full of racism year after year.

I once got a shirt that had a Nazi swastika on it. It was a red shirt with a great big white circle with the swastika boldly in the center of it. I did not wear it in front of my mother. I got it because of the cultural climate of American White biker types I thought I liked being around at that time. It transformed me within less than two hours that day.

I put it on and put the shirt I had on in the bag I got when I bought the shirt. I was pretty far from my house, all the way on the other side of town. Clifton, New Jersey, was where I spent most of my school years. I walked a little while around that side of town with it on.

It was a bright sunny day and beautiful outside, but inside myself, I did not feel beautiful at all. I felt dirty inside. I felt like the shirt was a disease on me, and by all accounts it was. Plus, it was against the core of my own beliefs that I had acquired by then.

But I did not even realize that when I bought the shirt. It took me wearing it to learn, and learn I did that day. That beautiful summer day, I became antiracist due to heritage. It was my two past histories of my birthplace plus my growing up place of the United States that turned me back to believing racism is wrong.

I'm German, and I know the history of Germany, with the Nazi Party trying to change the world in the twentieth century so drastically. The European culture of racism reached its pinnacle with Adolf Hitler paving the way for all the world to see the path of hatred and so-called supremacy. I had a shirt portraying its dirty symbol on my body, in front of my heart, and I could feel it for what it was: horrible.

The reason I could not wear it home was that my mom had grown up in that war. She and her family suffered from its existence around them.

All the homes around her were blown to pieces. Some of the daily chores in the community included digging out bombs that hadn't exploded, for fear they may explode and also to be used as scrap metal to exchange for worthless money to buy limited amounts of food.

Hunger was no stranger to my mother or her mom and brother then. My opa was in the military as a Nazi soldier because he had to be involved in order to survive. That also meant that he was not home to care for his children or wife during the whole war.

Mom told me many little stories of the war then. However, the two that stick the most in my mind still today are the ones about her being raped. She was first raped by a soldier of her own country who was of a low rank. I could feel her disappointment and sadness as she told me about this. Obviously, he was a criminal who used the war to continue committing his crimes while at war.

But the rape that affected her more was by an American lieutenant. He guided her into an alleyway with candy, some chocolate. This was a greater disappointment than the attack by the German soldier. The war was all wrong in many Germans' minds. And this lieutenant only made it even worse by her accounts because he represented a chance for the war to end. An answer to their prayers then.

The crimes were horrible by then. Most Germans wanted no part of the crimes being committed. They thought that the United States was going to help them against the enemy, which was supposed to be their own leadership: the Third Reich. To have a ranking officer from the United States do that opened her eyes to the sad truth that even the United States had its problems with leadership too!

So now you understand why I felt so dirty with that shirt on then. This adds another reason that I truly try not to be a racist, as I see the rest of the world can be. It is not easy to be antiracist with racism being so deeply etched into our culture. It is even harder to accept when you can't see the colors they speak of but feel the hate of all the years of false pride on both sides.

So, for me, I see purpose for peace in my views, from what I know of history within my family and of what I know in your families too.

Can I, or You, Stay Antiracist?

Well, I have a good foundation of it by now. But I will say it is not easy to stay that way each and every day. I'm very glad God has had me many days in His arms and heart because I also must keep Him in mine too.

I do think it is even harder today than it was many years ago. The reason I believe that is we were once divided by many ethnic groups before, even more so than we are today. Yet our country came together to help save the world from the racist ideals of the Nazi Party, which ended that oppression forever.

Where we are now is so damn politically divided overall by mainly two colors of this false divide. It's almost natural now for us to be two political parties of false races today. Hell, it's only politics, right?

No excuses. That is not how to be an antiracist or politically correct either. You either take responsibility for your actions and try your best to change, or you do not. If you need help, use the higher power available to us all. God loves attention from His children, especially when it comes to accepting His creation: you and the ones who are set separate from Him.

God knows hate because the devil was His creation before you. The hate that lives in the devil is his power as long as you give him rein. Racism is a devilish power. The devil's power will grow inside you if that is a power you desire to have. Satan has it in his mega storage in hell to give you. The will to have power above others at any cost as long as it serves you first is how he will lure you in. Is that your desire? Then hell is for you too. It is the knowledge of corrupting power.

I am very sorry that we have to change our trust in humankind into believing we ourselves are the only beings that make all change first. However, this has always been true from the beginning. Even in the Garden of Eden. One being led another being wrongly, only to believe that the knowledge gained was worth the cost.

Teaching the knowledge and hatred of racist views is an education of fools. That was the knowledge gained by racism, with our country having been led in its grasp from the beginning of the United States to today.

What I will always say and always believe to be true is God made us to be what we are: individuals. By being individual, you have the right to counsel but not the need to be misled by convictions or laws by politics that go against humankind. Yes, we must obey where and how we must by the law without breaking it wrongly. But following the simple Ten Commandments is the foundation of American law by our forefathers and should be our first choice to follow as well.

The Second Commandment by God states, "You should not make idols." That proves true in racism a million-fold when we examine history since racism's conception. We have had past citizens worldwide follow at great lengths leaders who were idols of the time. Those led by them committed many atrocities that should have never happened to anyone on our planet. All in the idea of following of an idol who led humankind wrongly.

Was God's law right then? And now, if we did this again? Yes, it is: no good being would do those type of things to another without committing a crime in the process, thereby breaking today's law too.

In the Bible, the ninth commandment states, "You shall not bear false witness against your Neighbor." Isn't that what racism is—an act of making another different by choices that are untrue? Does that commandment allow us to include a whole group with this false color to be labeled as we do?

No matter how they can try to argue a case against the ideals of an antiracist, the racist would lose the argument; if you stand to be antiracist, you will overcome racism every time. It is better to be on our own side with God at the helm rather than have a captain in racism lead you into hell, being their pawn.

What happens to one or many are not the doings of a whole. As a whole country, our design was always meant for unity and justice for all. It was designed to join the forces of minds, not powers. It was also designed to use God, as He is a guiding light to solving and managing our problems by using our own powers of reasoning to care for His creation, humankind. God has empowered every being to be exactly what an antiracist should be: His image in humankind.

11

POLITICS

The politics of "yesterday's" racism are, unfortunately, alive and well today. Those actions are still active, allowed, and accepted within many boundaries of society at large. Of course, one may ask, How can that be? There are many fewer people now reacting as poorly as we once did. In one sense, there is much less racist violence, sure. However, it is now so embedded into everyone's mindset that now the so-called Black and White populations of the planet know no other way to think.

Outside of racism, all things have evolved as they should. One major example would be television. That is the best example. What we once saw before in television, we no longer see now, and yet we still believe the politics of racism.

Our technologies since the creation of television have changed; however, the whole world around us regarding the politics of racism is still in the Stone Age.

Hate is blinding, and pride in the wrong things can really blind one's mind even more. Strange as it may seem, our minds have not yet caught up with technology. For if it did, our false colors would have faded away long ago.

When television was first invented, it was a marvel to the whole world. As it is today with the latest technologies, television was then too something that most of us could not even afford. But we all wanted it as soon as we could.

People would stand in store windows, watching a world they could only hear about on radio before television. We heard about important events on the radio first, and then we would flock together at storefronts to see it finally in black and white for ourselves.

These events were the talk of each and every town around the world, in the streets, taverns, supermarkets, workplaces, and everywhere we gathered together in groups. We talked and even quarreled about it all. This did not help racism back then either.

For the first time, other than through black and white illustrations, televisions across the world unfortunately amplified the idea of humankind being Black and White. What made things worse was that we still had major racial divides worldwide too.

America then had all too many moments of ignorance televised right there in front of everyone. It set into each and every one of us this difference of Black and White that even today is all we really see. It is hard now to not relate when speaking about another person of lighter or darker color without putting them into a racial divide. The concrete politics of our racial divide and demographics was set then as it is still today.

Of course, our technologies have evolved since then, and many laws have even changed. Even television changed to become what we all know and love—now it is in color—but people haven't changed.

Well, that is the politics of racism, folks: ignorance that has had no technological advancement since its conception. Why is that? Because it is hardwired into the fabric of our minds, hearts, laws, and politics of everyday life, and just about every one of us are embroiled in it.

People should have evolved with television once it changed. The old saying that still survives today, "colored people," should have evolved too because we are all colored in our own unique, individual way, just the way evolution or God has made us. And that color is truly only our skin tones. The real color of a person is their character, not their skin.

We are all being used each day in racism because we perpetuate it with our culture and politics. We have been sadly mind-controlled from when we were children by ignorance as we watched the world react again and again the same way, reinforcing that there is a difference between us.

So now our children learn just as we did, because the chain of racism is still not broken. But when does it start for us as people? It did not start in kindergarten because there are no politics for a child to learn yet. However, as the years progress in elementary school, so does their learning.

After kindergarten comes first grade and beyond. This is where we start to learn how we divide. We were taught to listen more, and we did just that. Our social skills are developing and, way before we leave elementary school, we become part of the divide and accept that we are of different races.

Even at home, our social skills change as we progress through those elementary years. All because we learn to listen. We listen to our parents, our friends, and the media. The whole world changes before our eyes to these lies where we are different from one another because of this thing called Racial difference.

My own father almost convinced me of racial difference. I will say my mother did her best not to go that way most of the time, but nonetheless, the chips even fell that way for her as well a couple of times.

Remember, a family is where we all learn, first and foremost. Next, the world around us sets ideas in even deeper once we venture there. And law, that great institution that is meant to guide us into living together as a society—look at what monumental work that has done to us over time.

I find law very fascinating because the facts can be altered by this simple but complex thing called norms. Racism really is a norm in our world. And these racist norms have been used as facts to alter law.

How the hell does that happen? Facts should be a real, tangible thing beyond what we think we see. On the front cover of this book, there are those who think they see a dog instead of a horse. Perception is what it is, but I tell you, the drawing is of the latter. Left unaddressed, false conclusions could continue for generations, as with the canine fallacy. Well, in terms of racial division, the argument by now has not only been accepted but also set in stone that we are of different races—even in our laws. I believe they keep the wording vague deliberately, to drive us apart.

When I reviewed most laws in regard to color differences, I noticed that they have written them so as to never be accountable for the law or government to be sued because of an outside argument against their law.

This is very smart on their part, and it should help most of us understand that even they realize there is bullshit in the game.

My wife was a labor attorney. She also ran an anti-discrimination firm for ten years. Of course, to be honest, the firm fought for Black people mostly and, in some cases, other nationalities which were discriminated against. My wife never mentioned any White people who needed the firm's assistance.

So, what I would surmise is the firm she worked for saw a great market to earn money in this matter, which the laws supported. Because the fact was that people were being mistreated and deserved help for discrimination. Her firm, I am sure, had great earnings to compensate their efforts on their plaintiffs' behalfs, of course. That was their niche in the great market of racist law.

Affirmative action refers to laws that protect us from the discriminatory actions of employers. Though they write these laws to also protect the government in its wording about Black and White, I assure you. Because of laws like these, we are forced into the mindset that we are of different races. Not by scientific facts but by racist norms around the world.

No matter how you slice or dice the law today, it includes a form of racism twisted throughout it, and you will find racism intended to encourage and manage a Racial Divide. Now because of my wife's expertise and degrees in law, she is a rock-solid White person in her own mind. She and I have had our debates on the matter. Of course, because my expertise is more about color as in art or sight, I seem insane to her. All I can say is, Sorry, I will not lie about what I do not see. There are no Red, Black, White, or Yellow people.

However, I would like to point out one real truth that plagues us today in too many ways. Whites of education and stature hold their Whiteness because of how they are still evolving today. This is especially true of many of the older ones who are holding on to their stature or power.

Just to let you know, discrimination happens to Whites too in workplaces around the world, even today. It even happened to my wife not too long back also. She lodged a complaint with her place of work when I was with her in regard to racism against and around her daily. As icing on the cake, it was ignored because the corporation did not wish an altercation on the matter. Instead, because of her age, they agreed on severance as a settlement to avoid any repercussions.

I would like to note that after knowing the whole event of her complaint and her Whiteness, I truly believe that she and her opposition were both guilty of racism in this matter. The unfortunate thing is that it also just shows us how Black and White many people are still being.

Those who lean toward so-called Black supremacy today are doing the same too. I get it—*we all have come a long way, baby*, to borrow that phrase. I also get that to struggle as a person labeled as something, you become proud of what you have accomplished, even if you are being labeled so falsely. So, you accept that label with some pride.

But the politics of racism are not about what you become if you can overcome your obstacles. They are about the division of humankind. They are about the segregation of our population, which is still being perpetuated by us all if we accept this continuum. As the world turns in the future, we will see more such continuums following. Because all those who are so proud of their own Whiteness or Blackness cannot let go of their own poor politics.

Those who are accomplished are worthy of their own doings, and rightfully so. But what none are worthy of is to hail their accomplishments as being a racially acquired ability. That is untrue and is also another continuum of nurturing racism further. It has been done before, and as long as we allow that type of behavior, it will lead others blindly again.

As unfortunate as it may be for many of us, we are too likely to follow another. Good leaders are very hard to find, because many live in this world's norm of the Racial divide. Our leaders need reprogramming, and it starts with the individuals who grow away from racism.

Each and every one of us is a seed—and we can all grow into leaders. That seed is very small alone. The mustard seed in faith is very much the same as our own and more than likely is why it is used in parables to teach faith.

Your heart and eyes are needed to win against racism. No mixed child should ever be gray because your heart is full of a past derived from hate or false stature. We are the seeds of a future that can change our leaders who wish and want to lead us rightfully. As we grow, they grow; as our mustard seed grows in us, they will begin to understand that change is long overdue. Once together, they will help us manage the many fields of humanity (like fields of grain that all grew from seeds).

The war of racism is not with weapons; it is with minds. If you have no war inside you that follows racism, then next shed your false color and join the whole Human Race again, like God and nature created. From there, let your seed be known and safe with you so that others may see the way.

A New Beginning

Probably the most important place to begin in the politics of racial divide is in a child's developmental stages (early years) of family and school. We are, in truth, now a very mixed society, so the divide between the ideas of races should be ending with our evolution of humankind.

The late John Lennon of the Beatles wrote a song called "Give Peace a Chance." That, for many of us older folks, should today remain a real catalyst to wake up to what he meant in that song about "Isms."

An Ism is politics, and racism is the largest of all Isms worldwide, for one reason or another. Politics can be very disruptive to a society. In fact, no matter where you turn in the world, you can see the results of disruption from one political problem to another. Even more sadly, in the United States, the greatest social disruption has been racism for over two centuries now.

With this fact in place, we have one of the greatest opportunities now to direct ourselves beyond the Racial divide today, not only in our homes but also in our schools. It is our job to voice the truth to our children and to our schools that the idea we are these false races is untrue.

Today, when registering a so-called biracial child in school, many families have a problem doing so. The registration application requires a parent to register their child as one race or another. But a biracial child is said to be two races due to the union of two opposing races, through no fault of their own.

There have been many families who have had this problem with the school systems' administrations nationwide, where to their frustration, they find the school will not accept a biracial registration. Plus, many systems will only allow that same family to register their child as BLACK.

Whether you realize this or not, that has gone on ever since the beginning of mixed children's lives. Racism has made the offspring of the world's mixed population BLACK out of disrespect for the parents' choice of being with each other as a mixed couple—in fact, there was a time where it was required.

So, pride has been a real part of this disruption of racism when we look at much of the news in our past. Recently, we had this group of people calling themselves the "Proud Boys," which caused a great stir of racial distraction in the news. It brought back White race politics and with it snowballed a landslide of consecutive results. The storm of protesters on the Capitol was part of that movement. Our President, Donald J. Trump, then lost his chance to be re-elected because of it. He foolishly became involved without ever realizing his mistake until it was too late to recover from it. Was he really part of their movement? Not at all. However, the rule of guilty by association applies here, does it not?

Then prior to that, we have had so many protests by those with pride bringing to their platform their own Black race politics, which has its snowball effect too. What starts to be a peaceful rally turns all too often violent with vandalism, robberies, and abuse of power against innocent bystanders.

Please note also these protests are fueled by what is too often thought to be Racial killings by police or citizens, which does nothing to prevent citizens to again become outraged over what should have never come to pass. Nonetheless, all these outcomes are fueled first and foremost by an aged old disease called racism and its politics that evolved over our past centuries till now.

It may be archaic, but it still plagues our entire planet today. We are no longer of that era, nor should we continue to teach our children or ourselves the poor politics of this Ism anymore. So, what better places to begin than our homes, in our families, and in changing our schools with the truth about the politics of racism.

Racism has no function that is good for any society. As a matter of history, it is quite the opposite. So, if we are going to make change, we should be honest in our politics and care for one another as a whole, not divided races of beings as we are now overall.

In no school should a political platform like racism be supported on any level. Due to the divides, not only do their minds become divided, but also it continues the platforms in our society. If a law were to be placed to learn proper behavior, it should be in a place where it can be learned by our youngest first. Then even our oldest will begin to change with the times as we progress with a system that no longer teaches there are separate races in our world or our schools.

There is no overnight fix, but in time, we will accomplish more good than bad if we make the change toward the truth. Also, the idea of justice for all will hold a greater meaning overall!

The times are changing, but to what? In the news today, there is this opinion of joining a Black with a Brown race as a combined group against their opposition. Is this the new wave of racism we need in our society? More than likely, we should assume no. Nevertheless, it is on the horizon. Just follow the news and the script that is unfolding before our eyes. A new fuel to the fire of racism begins.

Do people really want to be part of more of this? Probably not, because as we have seen, people who can be related to the idea of being a Brown Race have steered away from that type of thought for much of their life. Yet they have faced other types of prejudice toward their nationalities in ours and other societies around the world.

Hate and prejudice are forms of disruption the world will always face from the ignorant and narrowminded. It will always have a small hold on those who use it. But to those who do have the understanding of what they have gone through, may they begin to become enlightened. May they evolve as we all must too.

Each and every one of us must do our best to evolve from racism. This begins with a very simple truth. We have never been the color of a white page nor the black text upon it. We are simply a massive array of people who have a variety of flesh tones different from one another, only to help make us the individuals we are.

It is good to be human but wrong to not admit our mistakes. It is still and always will be wrong to have segregation. So why have we by law still allowed segregation to exist, dividing us into separate, false racist races? We divide no other creature upon our planet by some type of separate races or separate kingdoms. Nor should we do this to people unjustly.

12

A WHITE LIE

It is not that all of us claim to be created by God. Secular theories as to the origins of life are accepted by many as truth. This gives doubts to those believing in a God. The evidence of evolution presented to us is definitely a good argument for the nonbelievers, absolutely. Although if we go through much of our lives with these beliefs as true facts without faith, how do we allow others to twist our eyesight into believing we are colors that we are not?

Even still, there is in most of the world's mind more value to us to be created by a superior being like God, as our true creator. Because of that, we believe God empowered us to be in His likeness in some very important ways. He even gave us the ability to be creators of our own.

We can multiply ourselves as He did when He created us in His image. We can teach what He teaches, or we can choose to teach as we see fit for those we guide further. He gave us freedom to do as we can for our children and for humankind's future while we live here on earth. He made us free to make mistakes too! He gave us a chance of Divine right, and we have blown it tenfold over and over again with racism.

Of course, God never really wanted us to leave Him. As a result of our Divine right to freedom, we have and did stray away from even His leadership to manage our own leadership as we may wish.

Biblically, this began from the very start in Eden. A paradise made for us to be happy as God wanted us to live every day that we lived under His leadership. There He gave us freedom with one catch. We were never allowed to eat the fruit on the tree of knowledge. We were given a tree of knowledge but with no guidance as to how it would affect us if we chose to eat it without guidance by God Himself.

Well, a serpent lured Eve's attention and led her to believe that the tree of knowledge would give Adam and her the knowledge of God, making her believe this was good to have. She believed it to be true and then did the same as the serpent to lead Adam to the fruit on that tree. So, they tasted the fruit and thought this was great and believed what would come would give them all that was good and make them like God.

That completely changed everything in their lives at that very moment, and God proved it to them in a way that changed our entire world forever. They had knowledge they never really needed. They now knew good and bad. They now had things in their world that could make their lives difficult. They now had to become their own creators of all they needed. And now the world around them also needed to survive even if it had to devour them too. But their greatest lesson was to beware of what or who leads you toward harm.

For the most part, we know some of that truth. We have created so many things since then, good and bad. Our advancements in knowledge are leaps and bounds beyond everything we could have imagined from the onset. Humankind's creations seem endless for us. But with creations, too, come mistakes when things are made too quickly without the thought of possible outcomes.

Humankind has escaped most of its mistakes throughout time. Most mistakes are only talked about until those responsible are long gone. Then many are covered up with lies that are made to seem small and trivial. Plus, they are covered up by the next big thing to take your mind off the issue.

I cannot help but to go back to a memory when I was young with the idea of a white lie. It was a lie that was said to be almost nothing, just trivial.

Still, racism, in all honesty, is made by people who hailed themselves to be White people. Of course, they put themselves on top of all the races they created as if they were our god-like figures of knowledge for all humankind to believe.

This was hence a monumental "WHITE LIE," the largest and greatest lie of all time.

A white lie is defined as a harmless or trivial lie, especially one told to avoid hurting someone's feelings.

How the hell is that the case with racism? We have torn our lives apart as the one humankind God made in His image ever since it's been conceived. The birth of races is human-made only. It was created to lead and misled all under it. Yet it was done so without the truth ever being seen.

True color was in our lives before racism. How in this world does almost an entire planet not see that none of us are these false colors? The power of speech is absolutely amazing when it comes to humankind.

We have followed tons of leaders to our own destruction and keep doing it today, at this very moment. Then we pray to God for help about our stupidity of following others, ourselves, and our own sins.

Not one of us really fits this mold overall. The human form really is amazing when it comes to the individualities possible in us all. Yet still we are all so much as God said: we are made in His image too. Other words we are very similar.

Our differences are more politically divided by issues rather than having anything to do with separating us by false races. Within any of these races one can place us in, we are very much the same, one way or another. Yes, we pick sides, and the sides we pick have multi ethnicities mixed in. So how do you divide us by this race thing? It only exists because of racist people who have been misled by their own families and others.

I have spoken with many in the military who, when I talk with them about their race, they automatically say they are what the military keeps them divided as. I am White, that is what I am in the military, and that is it.

The same goes for others of these so-called colors. Again, the blind leading the blind. Every soldier is so much more and deserves so much more too.

They stand and fight next to a brother and sister in arms to protect them, not to protect the color that leaders make or frame us as. A soldier protects those who protect them too, and when doing this, they do not think about color. Race is irrelevant. Why? Because it is not really there.

And that is how racism can end. Racism really does not exist unless you choose to be misled and identify by its False Color Divide. The WHITE LIE is a lie.

Are You a White Lie?

If you were buying a product and chose a specific color, and received the right product but the wrong color, you would send it back, right? And if customer service insisted that a brown shirt was black, you would reject their claim, demand compensation, and walk away. Across the board, we cannot accept it if anyone tells us colors are not what we see—unless, of course, we have a disability of sight. But racism manipulates in this way. And as long as you live with it, you lie in it as well. It is your bed, so to speak. So do not complain of how you are slandered—that is who you choose to be.

Why not accept all the things others say that you can be too? That is utter nonsense, isn't it? As far as being molded into a group, we are not all the negative things others have done or do. The bad things anyone does are truly all their own, and those who follow together in doing wrong are still not the whole group either. However, they do fail and should face the same truth of their wrongs.

I am thankful that I can see I am not White, nor am I the race of White. I am even more thankful that I am not scared to call you wrong if you claim to be any of these false colors. Believe me, I have had many conversations on the subject, and everyone always ends up seeing the truth. So, when are you going to end the lie you live in? It is a choice and a responsibility of each of us to end this.

Thanks to all the mistakes by many of the so-called Whites of the past, few people of this False Color boast of themselves as being White. Many of them just don't do so. Why? Because inside their hearts, they are not the people of these mistakes, nor do they wish to follow them. However, one can inadvertently still support racism when one commits to writing that they are any of the colors of racism.

My birthplace is Germany, with one of the worst outcomes of racism and supremacies the world has ever seen since. I was born there. Does that mean I should be as them? Of course not! We all have freedom to choose how and who we want to be. I choose to be me first before anything or anyone else. Yes, my heritage is from there, but it is only where I was born, not where I evolved.

Each of us evolves as we are taught, guided, and wish to be. Each of us must always seek our own individuality and not be molded as a clone of another.

But there are still those who step out with the ignorance of boldly saying they are Whites or Blacks, and look at the results of that. The Capitol of the United States finally saw a backlash from the ignorance still haunting our country with racism. Our streets, homes, and businesses are still being vandalized and destroyed by others who boldly commit to using their false race as an excuse to do so, because sometimes only one being was wronged. But many can wrong others in their path of hate and racism in return.

This is shameful and worse yet, reinforces the idea that all those in that group embody the same stereotype of bad people. When the dust settles and all can relax from these altercations, we normally can look back and realize that not all are this way.

Most of us, that is. There will always be the few who hold their hatred and stir the pot till the heat boils over again for the next uprising. These are the baton wavers who lead us to failure in the Racial divide.

I am very sorry to say this, but we deserve to see our bold ignorance even more now than ever. Every country around the world is still bathed in the ignorance of racism, as if it is true that we are different races. No, that is a lie, just like supremacy is a lie that gets knocked down every time it gets too full of itself too.

I am sorry that many will hold on to these false colors no matter what. Many find it cool to be one of these colors. Even so, by doing this, they hold on to the racism they try to stop. Ask yourself this: If the divide and racism is right, why not recreate a party like the Nazis to end it all instead?

As far as being Black, please allow me to commend all those who have lifted up people by their great works to prove the slander is false. The stereotypes held now in their culture were forced upon them, embedding themselves into the way society at large perceives them. Unfortunately, stereotypes of this nature are very hard to change.

Let us laugh about this a little. So, we have the television channel BET, Black Entertainment Television, right? Imagine WET, White Entertainment Television. Really, WET TV, no that doesn't work, does it? Yet that was what television once was. That would certainly be a great inspiration for some comedy.

However, we do understand why a Black culture network evolved. It was influenced by the lack of diversity on television. Because of that, it is very understandable that it developed. But it continues their platforms of racism with its false color.

But really if someone did create that network, what would happen? You know what would happen right from the start. It would become a mass media interest against the whole idea of it. Wait—why? There is a network whose theme is Black television, so why not White television again. But boldly stating it is White is no different than the opposition.

What I am saying is there would be an opposition because racism exists, and this would only fuel the next complaint by a leader who could cause a revolt in some manner or another.

There was a time where it seemed like only one culture had rights here in the United States overall. Thank God the walls around that are falling down more and more every year that passes.

In other countries, the same thing exists but with different cultures at the helm in their dominions. In government it is an issue all the time to have an imbalance in its network as well, with the idea of racial differences. This is now changing more and more slowly over time.

But let us consider this a moment: Is it the imbalance of ethnicities or more the imbalance of truth that should be the issue at hand? Our system in the United States claims to represent truth and justice for all. This is not the case, many times over. The law is not the same for us all. There are changes over the course of history, maybe even some improvements. But due to our false divide, there remains a substantial imbalance.

If we are one nation overall, then let us strive to make it just that. If we are to do that, then it is the division of our people we should handle first and always. In our pledge, we say "indivisible." Then be indivisible. One nation, one Race. End racism by telling the truth about us: we are one, just as God has made us. We can stand together as one through all things with no more false racial divide.

The Challenge

Here lies a challenge for all nations, not just our own. Of course, I wish it would be ours first, but it probably won't be.

What nation in the world will end the racially False Color Divide before all others by first law and then actions? All around the world now, we have native inhabitants of almost every ethnicity known to humankind in the United States and in many other nations too. So there should be one nation with the guts to finally begin what God intended all along: a Human Race never alienated by its own.

May we, with God's help, guide our leaders to do so.

The Second Challenge

This is for all those so-claimed religious believers in their religions for their God. I am including you in this as well. It does not matter what faith you try to keep. Can you as a being change yourself and your church against racism and the False Color Divide?

In other words, will you and your church no longer lie and be part of the greatest WHITE LIE in the world? It is written in many religious books of God's feelings toward lies. He holds no favor for a liar, so how can He hold favor in a church of liars?

An example of a lack of favor toward a religious group or community, we could assume, shows in their realm of where they live and the blessings they do not receive thanks to their own ignorance. There are countries in ruin and yes, they are ruled by those who are ruthless. They lead their own people to ruin, make their people their pawns to kill their fellow citizens if they will not accept their way to live.

Our beliefs are our core. We have a right to believe as we will but also do not have a right to impose our beliefs on our fellow citizens. Take away that core of one's being, and we begin to fail and behave very differently when our backs are against the wall, striving to live by another person's beliefs. We see it everywhere; even here in the United States, there are communities in ruin.

End the lies of false color, and open not only your own eyes but also the eyes of all those you love and share with. A church is just that—a place we share together and a place where we leave all lies outside, away from Him and our people alike.

My Promise

I promise to do just that. I write not only to share change with each reader but also to change the very house I chose to learn more about God from always and forevermore.

Racism began in one house and spread like a disease, no different than any other. Its only cure is one of honest sight. And with the blessings of every willing person to finally agree they have been led wrongly, we can change.

13

CHILDREN TORN BY DIVIDE

Cultural differences matter only to those who make them a divide. However, these types of divides in relationships create deep faults within the caverns of our memories in many of us. This starts from a very young age.

I have felt this divide culturally all my life and have seen it in others who are either a mix of two different nationalities, a mix of two different statures of society, or so-called different races.

For me, this divide has caused much mental anguish. I have seen the same thing across the board in many others, who have had the same divisional problems thrown at them growing up. I will give some examples so that we may try to find a solution. Even so, the answer is different for each of us based on our own experiences.

Binational Marriages

In the binational relationship, people of two different nationalities have fallen in love, and it is wonderful for them. They have a rock-solid foundation called love. This was the way of the world for most marriages of those who met beyond their borders or within. One example is love found overseas during military employments. That creates an opinion of differences thanks to each partner's standards colliding, especially with their families colliding over their union together as well.

This is happening every day still, but our futuristic societies now find it easier to permit us to divorce one another more quickly, which helps lessen the amount of time they all endure their conflicts.

These conflicts in some ways are all too common, and they can create great disparities, hence affecting a child with a separation of cultural differences too. The standards of each parent become an issue a child has no way of understanding or even a wish to try.

Being binational in the United States should, in fact, be culturally acceptable, we would think. Especially as we are a nation joined together by means of migration and immigration from around the world. However, each of us has our own internal cultural differences within the variety of perspectives found in the U.S. and our family's ancestral views of stature shared at the dinner table.

There are three listening areas in which a child hears their families' differences. The three living spaces are the dinner table, behind closed doors, and the living room, where the outside world gets reviewed by all in the family together.

At the dinner table, most of us are fortunate because the conversations are usually not too filled with bad views and contempt of the world. However, bring to the table views of social disruption, and a meal can taste less delicious at those times, and Mom's good cooking can be forgotten.

Most parents try to keep their differences from the kids behind closed doors. But the walls tell all when parents speak too loud. A loud complaint about cultural differences is almost always heard, and when a child hears it, it only creates confusion for them. They don't know what side to take because they are a mixture of both sides. They now can feel unbalanced from the differences of their parents, which slowly can affect their own thinking one way or another. The living room is a place we can stay together with a mixture of world views added to a child's imagination about how the world works according to their parents' views. What a mess that can be.

The news depicts worldwide topics that the media slices and dices to make them appear to be more eventful than they should be for our home. Then thanks to its hype, Dad or Mom follows it with their views, all too often out loud.

Television was a center of attention for all kinds of human behavior and faults. Movies, TV series, variety shows, and documentaries all show a child the faults and sarcasm in the world around us, often with some added comment from their parents' view to top it off. I can remember more than I ever wanted to hear or know at times about their views.

I am this child. Both my parents as far as I am concerned are great. You cannot make me dislike or hate either one. But their views because of their personal ignorance and perspectives influenced me with their faults—and my faults, later in my life. Granted, I was raised during civil unrest and some of modern media's first attempts at enraging False Division.

My cultural divides were a lot to try to understand or decipher growing up. I had to be cautious with my pride for either side of my family. It was often very difficult to manage. Sometimes I think I was the cause of an argument or two because of the mixed views inside me that came out naturally. I thought my family's views were open most of the time. Sometimes I would express mine too!

Apart from my experience, this dynamic is a mistake for many children. It puts us on a fence between two of the most influential people in our world: our parents. This fence rides the line along the divide between their differences. And there we are, acting and reacting amidst the two of them bitching and arguing with each other during current and social events—all of which have nothing to do with them.

Their differences are just like many others. There are the differences of stature, nationalities, and beliefs in hierarchy, which is probably one of the worst of them all. Because what follows all too often is some supremacy.

Then there are the religious views, which can be different too, and they were. Religion has been one of the biggest reasons people have adjusted their boundaries.

The most significant point of view that caused a big impact and confusion had to do with the racial divide. Growing up, I saw riots on television that were caused by issues of the Black and White differences in society. At that time, there were far too many. Plus, television back then was in black and white. This made people look Black and White, almost as the media were trying to depict them.

However, I could see when I stood next to somebody else that none of us were these colors. Only on television and in debate with everyone around the world would I hear about the idea that we are separate races.

Well, there I was going to church with my mom, learning about God, about the whole creation story, and the Ten Commandments. And of course, today, I find a lot of irony in how I was raised to believe it was a tough world to grow up in, with these beliefs in one's heart to boot! Nonetheless, what I always took home with me from church was the message that we are God's children before we are our parents' and that He made one humankind in His image, not two, three, or four.

That being true, there is only a God, one of Him, and only one humankind in His image. The one and only one Human Race.

Two Levels of Society Marriages

Now a marriage between two different statures of society creates many different opinions in a household, as you can imagine. In these marriages, children face a wide variety of issues based on differences of cultural stature, putting them on a fence between the opinions of their parents and those that their families could have of one another.

These issues are not any easier for them either. Because in their world, they see a divided stature that makes one side lowly and the second raised above the other. But the child only sees love for both and experiences feelings of confusion between their most loved idols: their parents.

Supremacy is a really hard issue to have imposed upon a young viewer. It can have effects that trouble a child for the rest of their life if it makes them the lesser. It can also teach them to be disrespectful to other people if they are not taught that respect is earned, not a privilege. I have seen the aftermath, and it is hard to overcome. Privilege or improper respect; they can turn out to be somewhat the same.

The greatest damage of all is that it can set a child's mind toward a platform of supremacy that they may carry against others as well. This is usually in the form of the blame game, which no one ever wishes to hear but must from those who can be judgmental against others. The mimicry of self-righteousness and learned behavior is carried down to the next generation.

Remember that it was the leaders in Europe who created racism and made themselves supreme. The elite were hard to satisfy then and have never changed, even to this day. Supremacy is the foundation of racism.

If you are part of a supremacist group, they accept you till you don't accept them. Denial is always apparent when guilt is thrown back—at every level.

Interracial Marriages

What a wonderful mix it should be. Marriage should unite the divided, and there should be a harmony between each party, and in some cases, that does occur.

However, all too often, the world around the two parties in an interracial marriage has issues with their marriage. Many times, much more than they expect. Plus, remember at one time that it was so taboo that families disowned both parties in the marriage and even the children along with them.

It is about love, of course. There is the attraction of their differences. Plus, today it is widely accepted by most of us, or is it? It is and it is not. That is the problem a child faces more than adults because they must grow up in the midst of it all—their ears being filled with it throughout their childhood.

Racism is thriving, and with it, the divide grows deeper with every movement. Each event separates us and them racially. We have to remember that racism is a form of oppression, which is a great weight upon a child's heart, soul, and mind.

Within the household of these mixed children, they can face many odds. Usually this is not their own doing, but nonetheless they can feel as if it were their own fault at times.

These issues are mixed as perhaps they should be overall, but this should not mix up the child's mind to the point of confusion about their own identities. But of course it does and also can slow down their own will to thrive as themselves. Because they become too often stuck on the nonsense others speak wrongfully.

A mixed child by so-called Black and White people does not make them one race or the other. Nor does it make them gray by mixture either. However, it does make them a milestone of truth in the biracial discussions, disputes, protests, riots, and legal arguments: that none of us are these false colors created by a past history of hate and supremacists in the world.

In truth, we are all a mixture of two parents whose origins are different from one another. As our parents are both individuals, so are we individual. Never should we be raised to be divisible to or by humankind other than regarding our own identity. Because each of us is unique, as our DNA proves.

Another point that should be addressed thanks to the ignorance of racism is that these children have also been falsely titled. If there is no legitimate proof of multiple races, then these poorly accused children, as citizens, are being slandered by their own country and the world we live in.

14

PRIDE

I have it and have not had it. Have I ever had White pride? Well, I cannot tell you I have. I have had that cross my mind in my life, when I was younger, only to realize at that time that it never was portrayed in my families as a merit to have—so why should I?

I do see so many have pride. People have made it evident throughout my sixty years of life. Of course, we look at the poorest portrayal with the beginning of what was slavery and much of American history from the earliest point to now. We also see this with the Nazi campaign in world history, hailing their superiority across Europe.

One thing I wish to point out is slavery was not started here in the United States. Nor was it Black slavery at first either. In each journey across the Atlantic in our early history, someone was a slave to another on the ride across the water.

As a point of racist divides, almost every newcomer came with a new social divide with airs of supremacy against them, or also as they saw against another. Such was the way of the social history of racism or ethnic pride in the beginning of the United States. The wops, the micks, the gooks, and so forth. The terms are endless when it comes to slander, disdain, and hatred. And new ones are thought up again and again, even today.

Pride is maybe a good thing to have for the right reasons, and that pride helps keep one's chin up. The hard worker deserves it. Because they are driven to doing and getting a job done well. A good-hearted individual has it not because they like or need to brag about it but because it is their natural state of mind and being. They are just good people who are that way.

A leader's pride shows by how they lead another. Some do not overrate themselves or state they are above another. They lead by staying on the course of business at hand without wavering one way or another. Their point is spot on to the direction they lead, and they are not doing it to mislead anyone. They will step beside those they lead with the will to do what they ask. They will also do it without making a point to show fault to those who they are in charge of. We learn best from these types of people overall too.

To continue this on the alter ego of pride, it can be very misleading. This pride can have disdain for others with sarcasm, ridicule, hatred, and much, much more. This type of pride shows that the ones it is aimed at are much less. That they are the ones who those must follow, and they are uniquely something far different than those they oppress. Sound like anything you know in the past? Perhaps an emperor or even Hitler? Or many of our present-day politicians.

If we were to look at recent history, this is what many have faulted our President Trump for. It was easily surmised by many actions both on his part and others who followed him and exhibited even worse behavior. Did Trump, his so-called followers, and anyone happy to point fingers realize anything as to how all of us have been led wrong? Probably not.

Today I live in Georgia, where, at the time of writing this, our election was being redone because of problems with vote counts. There is a candidate running for Senate who is using his leadership skills to sway the vote his way. This election will be done in a couple of weeks from now.

This election is being done because of ballot discrepancies from the first run. The votes were too close, so they are redoing it.

For example, this candidate is known for his manner of speech on the podium in church before others who listen to him. Today in the news, he called on the U.S. "to repent for its worship of 'Whiteness'" over the success of President Trump's candidacy.[2] That there was a direct accusation that most of America is guilty of racism. This same man is very much guilty in his own part of stirring up his congregation on racial issues.

I am sure there may be some good intentions in his will to lead. However, the U.S. as he stated is not one type of citizen; it is many types. His statement creates an even larger wedge in the diversity of the United States.

He has also been known to say that God should "DAMN" America. He is a preacher of GOD'S WORD. He is there to help God's people to understand the WORD of GOD, not do GOD'S job to damn a nation or its people.

God in the Bible damned His archangel and in doing so, God gave this angel a dominion of a place none of us wish ever to truly go. This was who we now know as Satan, the king of hell and all who go there.

The devil also can have his powers within those who allow him in their hearts and souls here on earth too, if God allows it. Biblical history shows God allowed the devil to test Job's faith in Him. The devil did, and Job was not swayed. Are you swayed by the devil in you with Satan at your helm?

Does God allow the devil to do that? Yes, because this is his dominion also by God's will. But fear not; we have a choice to follow who we will.

Humankind does not need another devil. Nor does any country need to be damned by one of God's people of leadership. I cannot say what God will do for Rev. Raphael Warnock, but I do know God will not follow his leadership and damn us by his rhetorical passions.

Plus, we are all guilty of following a past of racism without understanding its misrepresentation of leadership. But a preacher of God should not stand in the racist past, nor keep lying in the pool of false statements about this false color platform.

Here is a very interesting point about where Rev. Raphael Warnock preached his services before becoming a senator for Georgia. His church is

---

[2] Rev. Raphael Warnock, "How Towers Tumble" (Sermon), Emory University, October 2016

the very same church our great Martin Luther King, Jr., served his parishioners. I think it is sad this man dishonors our late leader Martin Luther King, who helped so many of our people to a better nation.

If God is not enough for those who follow Him, then God is not their idol. Meaning we are the idol we choose instead of God first. For this choice, those who do are guilty of breaking the Second Commandment.

Pride is a tool that can misguide those who follow praise falsely given among themselves. So, has it been in the praises of racism? Many so-called Whites have been guilty of it. Even so, we should give thanks that many no longer ever wish to be ever considered White again. Those that do continue the idea of White Supremacy are considered bad people by many societies around the world. Is this not rightfully so in most of our sights and hearts? I hope and believe this is so.

Now this is the hardest part for me to write about, and I will do it with as much care and respect as I can. I say this because I have great respect for all people overall. The people made by racism to be so-called Black across the globe faced so much, and I cannot apologize enough to make up for what has happened in the world's history. Nor are we responsible today for the actions of others from their past, because we had no part in it.

Africa has had a history of disruption by their own humankind before ours. From one end of their continent to the other, the inhabitants of Africa's greatest threat has been humanity and still is today. But those who threatened their survival were those in power nearest to them first.

First were the predator tribes with warrior spirits and ways. This part of their lives was difficult enough. But then came the conquerors from far-off worlds. These conquerors had evolved differently and believed they were better, smarter, and deserved to have power over those they considered to be less than them at the time.

Of course, on the continent of Africa, there were these great leaders of that continent first, like the Egyptians, and there were others, too, who tried to enslave the lesser evolved of their world. They would conquer small tribes to enslave them to build their kingdoms. Egypt is one the greatest wonders of the world, showing how the power of kings and slaves can accomplish so much.

Did the kings always go out to enslave others? No, they sent out their own soldiers to police their kingdoms first and enslaved any violators of the kingdom's law. Their pride was to control their kingdoms and people. Not a very nice way to serve their people; however, it was the way of the times then.

They paid for the rest of their slaves from outsiders who brought them to their kingdom. These people who were conquered were from other tribes across their continent.

These people were often natives whose tribes were peaceful. They were satisfied with what they had. Their greatest predators were other tribes, warrior tribes that conquered small tribes to sell them for weapons and goods to advance their own glory.

One such tribe had the simple pride of caring for their own by peacefully coexisting. Another tribe had the pride of conquest; they saw value in conquering their countrymen for simple commodities. This world still exists in Africa today in many places. Of course, today much of it is done very differently and much more secretly than when it was done in open markets.

There is this little girl in the United States to whom I wish to give some praise. She is only eight years old and started a company. She is her own CEO of a line of dolls, books, and accessories. Her name Zoe Oli. Her mission is to empower girls of color with her company Beautiful Curly Me.

I saw her on the news saying that she was creating her stuff to be "BROWN like me." I found this statement innocent, honest, and absent of racism. Little Miss Zoe makes any and all of my efforts worth aiming for because of her unadulterated opinion. Also, because she must have two very amazing parents who support her efforts of honesty. My respect goes out to both Mr. and Mrs. Oli.

However, we also know she is young, and all her company's editing is being done for the most part by adults very close to her. When reading about her company's products, you will find that the brown of her eyesight as to her perceived color is no more. This is not her fault at all; she is amazing as she is now. This is not the fault of the editing but more a fault of us all for continuing to support our racist ideals in society today.

But the dialogue is the idea that her products depict the Black race instead of her own self-perception. Her pride is pure and absent of racism. I admire her vision and honest sight. May she see the world as it really is: a colorful place with many people of different colors, not false colors.

I understand completely how and why Black pride has evolved. I wish I could have a small part of their enthusiasm to what they are uniting to believe in. But if I was to do so, I would have to accept the concept and realization that it makes me part of the bad parts of the past too.

Can you as a Black individual accept that continuing to teach your own that any of your bad past has a value worth celebrating as being a false color. Maybe one should consider the worth of a pride based upon a past molded by false ideals.

Every history has riots, vandalism, wars, civil unrest, and divide due to these types of disturbances. Is this what we are? It is our past! I beg you to not believe you are the past false race forevermore. Be as your family today, not the families of our past mistakes.

If you are a believer of God, then believe that our likeness to Him is not a color that was designed to make each of us different in ways He has chosen for us to be. I can assure you He made us to be uniquely different in every possible color of skin. He could design us to be, as individuals.

Certainly, have pride for oneself without boasting to a point of Racial divide. For we are in the view of the world around us that can change with one another's help.

We are a country whose past heritages come from around the globe to join themselves to a people who claim freedom from the enslavements that hold others in the world down.

We must have **PRIDE** but not pride in what does not need to be celebrated falsely in division. We must become what we once said we were: indivisible once again in order to end racism in the United States or anywhere else in the world.

Our sight is not blind. Our minds are clear when we are not being misled. We know truth is something that can never be twisted by itself. We know that people before us have been told to believe what is not true; even our forefathers themselves were led wrongly. That is why they came to create a new nation.

Be proud; be who you are alone. For you alone can end the pride of false color first before another. Be the individual you are, and let no being tell you otherwise. Your wisdom is as great as any other if you choose to be honest first.

Honesty is our best policy. Live against racism by being the antiracist who sees all racism is wrong.

15

CAN WE MANAGE CHANGE?

There is no easy way when it comes to change, especially when it comes to the massive era of racism. For one reason or another, change is friction in the wheel of life's motor. Nonetheless, we are very fortunate to be living in an age with the technologies we have now.

The motor of society moves much more quickly, thanks to the internet. Now social media is directly in everyone's hands on our phones. Our society is already primed for the changes that are about to come. Still, what will those changes do to us if we keep following leaders with an intent that goes against one another as a whole?

All these centuries of racism bring a very long history of ignorance to repair. We know it cannot be repaired. Let us face the truth at hand: people today are much more ready to accept what we see more than what we cannot, along with the idea that none of us are these colors, which is pretty simple to see up front.

Plus, as an asset, there has been a history of great feats of character in every facet of nationality across the globe. No one can truly ever say that one nationality cannot do what another can do any longer. Because next, there will be another from some other ethnicity who will do it even greater one day, proving to all that no being's will has boundaries other than their own to surpass.

The last people in our society to accept this will be those Americans who wish to hold on to their ill-gotten concept of color. Which means that there will be some of the two false races of Black and White who will hold on for decades, whether the law changes or not.

For these people, we should try our best not to become overzealous about their hold on what has been their mainstay for generations, both for them and their past generations of family who led them there. Our family bonds are our trust, and in our families, we have lived as these so-called races even if they were false. So, continue to love and honor those of your past, but do not follow in the footsteps that lead to their mistakes.

We must take a stand of truth openly, without fear of any reprisals. Our system was actually built on just that concept. Believe me, even with that being said, there will be many political figures confused about the issue of changing it all, because they will need to change the mold of what they thought they represented before this change. The honest ones will not have much trouble because it is why they originally wanted to become leaders. To do right for all.

It will change very quickly once it catches on, and it will be even more important that we do our best to show one another that we are truly fellow native Americans once and for all.

The United States and the world need us at our best, and that cannot happen until we beat down the foundations of racism overall in American law first. The only Black and White that should ever exist from now on is the white of a page and the black of text or whatever is true by its own color.

We need to lobby our political leaders to sway them to making this change with us. We need to boldly show our support for change among ourselves and publicly. We need to stand up in our churches and finally declare to God our mistakes with one another. And promise to be at one another's side as God is for us when we need Him.

There are many who are ready for this change, and they too feel the same over these issues of racism. It is unbelievable that it has existed as long as it has.

Racism has beaten down the oppressed and lifted up their uprisings. We no longer have a need or desire to oppress our fellow Americans, nor do we as a whole population wish to do it elsewhere around the world. People have evolved and are ready for change.

Be once and for all an honest individual who believes it is right to be a citizen who is indivisible once again when it comes to being American. Also believe we are only one Race of the whole world, not just the United States. Yes, we are human, and in our past, we allowed the idea of racism in our laws beyond our reasoning as well as individuals beyond our influence.

As a nation, we may be guilty of not changing this mess sooner; however, now one by one, we will change our way ahead.

Now you have been more enlightened to a truth that many have kept away from us for hundreds of years. Let this not be up to our babies to make this change. It should be up to us all as soon as we can finally evolve away from the ideas of dividing our Human Race with such foolish thoughts.

We must be very proud of those trying to pave the way now in sports and entertainment against racism. This journey for Americans is only just beginning. The road ahead will have its bumps along the way.

The most important place in our lives will be in our homes and families. For those of you who have trouble with change, we all have faith that change is coming. May it come peacefully to you and your family as well.

As for the politicians of our country, all we can hope for is that they accept the truth before them. Honesty is what they claim to possess, and this we will see in our future too. We need our leaders to change. We need our leaders to remold themselves before they ever try to remold us again against one another. We need our leaders to not use our mottos to mislead us by saying In God We Trust when they really mean may God help you because I cannot or will not.

The most important motto to follow should henceforth be "Truth and Justice For All."

"No More False Color Divide."

We are individuals who can be indivisible and proud of being one Human Race.

16

THIS IS FOR ALL THOSE WHO
HAVE DIED DUE TO RACISM

It is and will forever be an honor to honor those who have died. They may have died for reasons of bravery or slavery. They may have died in our streets due to differences of hate or fate. They may have died because of poor leadership or jobs that were done wrongly by those misled from their convictions of what they know or do not know. But they will always be a part of our minds to remind us that we do care that they died and that they are missed by those who are left behind.

We will continue to change, always. We will continue to have differences, always. We are all different in some significant way, whether it is DNA being the most individual divider or the effects of each individual in our society today.

I had a recent conversation with a gentleman next to a client I had in a home improvement project. I think you will find his reaction to our conversation to be true. I was talking to him about what I was writing now in this book about our racial divide. He was obviously a person who loved motorcycles, a past veteran, a so-called White man with many tattoos, and he was retired from a job he had had for thirty years. This description is to help you envision the character. His nickname was Cowboy, and this was in Georgia.

So, I told him the book's title, "The False Color Divide," and that we are not these colors of RED, BLACK, WHITE, or YELLOW. His response was a perfectly correct statement in a manner and tone that I must share again. So, he said, "Yeah, I know we are not 'FRICKIN CRAYONS.'"

It made me smile as we laughed and talked for a bit longer. The conversation stuck in my mind all night, and I got to see him again the next day as I completed the job next door to where he lived. I told him I would use his words in this book in our next conversation before I left.

So, to those who have died, I want us all to remember we are certainly so much more than what we are framed to be from our past history as divided colors in what ignorance, hate, supremacies, or politics have molded us to be. It was never correct to mold us into a box of "FRICKIN CRAYONS."

To those who have died due to racism, we owe it to them to change our platforms of racism and end the idea that we can be what we are not.

We need to take a stand together as one Race, as we are only human. And finally make this statement:

"I Stand as an Individual, Indivisible, One God, One Race, and Human only." But to those who do not believe in God, just omit Him as He will omit you also. Also, it will take a long time, but as time goes on, we can teach not only our children honestly but also one another and ourselves in the future.

Let us tell not only our people as citizens but also our governments that we are only equal as long as the law states the truth about us all. And may the world one day soon follow with equality as one Race without false colors to separate us by law or humankind ever again.

Then all those who died from or in our one Race's racial divide will have not died in vain. Plus, for all those who stand as racists, may their efforts to divide our world like Nazis fall to ruin forevermore.

We are worth all that poor leadership uses us for, but we were never meant to be misled by supremacy. The continuation of our False Divide will mean that allies who have fallen, did so in vain. If you truly have any respect for your own ancestors, you will stand with us all together as one.

Racism's End

Happiness is freedom from racial division for all humankind.

Together, we are One Race.

These two young boys face a future where they will be taught that they are framed by racism. And because of racism, they will be told by many they're BLACK because they had two parents who were also framed to be the false colors of racism. One Black, the other White.

Then they will be taught that by racism it is said they are biracial because of the mixture of their parent's false races. With that knowledge of ignorance made by humankind, not God, they will also be told that racism cancels out their mother's so-called race. Does this happen because only the father's race matters? No, it does not.

When they are able to understand, they will be told the truth: Racism has an ignorance that only allows them to be Black because the so-called

White will not accept them any longer as their own in the Supreme Race. Also, because most biracial children bear some resemblance to the so-called Black race.

This is the way of racism. It is also the way that people made this conception alone by only thought and mental theory of their time. These people were thought to be great leaders of knowledge and worth believing. All this happened over five centuries ago with no medical or scientific proof.

Over the time of racism's own evolution, the thought went a little deeper than thought alone because of fossils discovered that seemed to show that some of humankind evolved to become separate species from prehistoric man. Of course, ignorance still played the larger part of the equation then too.

Hence the framing of racism. In their ignorance, their theories were about human beings evolving from apes, but within that theory, they also then framed the separate idea there were separate races. The most ignorant part of those theories was that the Black race was the one that evolved from apes.

Now thanks to the knowledge of DNA and genes, we know there is no definitive proof of separate races. There is proof of heritages and origins but not of any racial divide.

This really is wonderful news for all the believers of religious text. It helps certify the text of biblical writing that God made His image as being not only one like Him but also only one humankind.

It is said that idle hands may do the devil's work. If that can be true, then another biblical truth comes to play in the form of racism also. According to biblical text, the devil has dominion of earth since he was sent here.

If that be so, imagine his part in the whole scheme of RACISM! He was a mastermind of all the acts of racism to keep humankind from believing in God and to believe in the leadership of human beings first.

It sure has worked well for a very long time. However, his work in racism ends now with me and my two grandsons from this day forward. It also ends with every child I know who is framed as biracial, which I can proudly say there are many who bless me and those around us too.

From this days forward, all those who are framed in the lie of racism no longer need to believe the idols of racism. Nor do they have to be or take part in the world's mistake in the "FALSE COLOR DIVIDE."

Made in the USA
Columbia, SC
29 January 2025

52506267R00067